Sydney

A guide to recent architecture

•••

Francesca Morrison

Sydney

A guide to recent architecture

● ● ● ellipsis **KÖNEMANN**

• • •

Sydney: a guide to recent architecture

CREATED, EDITED AND DESIGNED BY
Ellipsis London Limited
55 Charlotte Road London EC2A 3QT
E MAIL ...@ellipsis.co.uk
WWW http://www.ellipsis.co.uk
PUBLISHED IN THE UK AND AFRICA BY
Ellipsis London Limited
SERIES EDITOR Tom Neville
EDITOR Annie Bridges
SERIES DESIGN Jonathan Moberly
LAYOUT Pauline Harrison

COPYRIGHT © 1997 Könemann
Verlagsgesellschaft mbH
Bonner Str. 126, D-50968 Köln
PRODUCTION MANAGER Detlev Schaper
PRINTING AND BINDING Sing Cheong
Printing Ltd
Printed in Hong Kong

ISBN 3 89508 645 2 (Könemann)
ISBN 1 899858 33 4 (Ellipsis)

Francesca Morrison 1997

Contents

Introduction

Sydney's icons, the Harbour, the Harbour Bridge and the Opera House, are internationally known, but the work of only a few of Sydney's architects is recognised outside Australia. The practice of architecture flourishes in Sydney, but, due to the geographic isolation of the continent (and despite the great advances in communication technology), active participation in the international exchange of ideas and theories, which stimulates and underpins world architecture today, is the exception rather than the rule. Consequently, debate is more oriented to specific urban and regional issues than to theoretical ideas, and architecture has been generally more concerned with addressing particular problems and expressing a regional identity than with being at the cutting edge of internationally recognised design.

Sydney is a dynamic city, and this is reflected in its buildings, with many innovative projects that are forging an identity for the city, and many architects who are deeply involved in its development through the making of a meaningful and expressive architecture. This guide will introduce to the reader just over 100 buildings completed since 1985. It will give some understanding of the state of architecture in the city and will reveal something of its culture and the concerns of its citizens.

With 3.5 million inhabitants, Sydney is not a large city in terms of population. By area, however, it is immense, covering 10,000 square kilometres, though much of this is suburbia, sprawling north and south along the eastern seaboard and penetrating as far west as the Blue Mountains. There are 45 local councils in the Sydney Metropolitan Area, which extends from Campbelltown, 50 kilometres to the south west, as far as Gosford/Wyong, 80 kilometres to the north. The centre of population of this megalopolis is deep in the western suburbs (the site for the 2000 Olympics is well related to it), about 20 kilometres from the city centre, which, itself, remains compact on its harbour setting and is the site of much of the new architecture.

Metropolitan Sydney is a water city. With 100 kilometres of ocean beaches stretching the length of the coastline, Sydney Harbour at its centre, and half a dozen rivers with their bays, inlets and tributaries forming a vast network of interior waterways, the city is well endowed with idyllic water environments. This allows great numbers of people to live on or close to the water's edge, or to enjoy water views. Living near the water is important to Sydneysiders, and is a factor which has had, and is still having, a tremendous effect on the city's development through its reinforcement of suburban rather than urban values and lifestyles.

Sydney's first European settlement was founded on the harbour, at what is now Circular Quay, by Captain Arthur Phillip on 28 January 1788, and since that day, Sydney Harbour has been considered the city's major asset. (Practically every Sydneysider will ask the visitor what he/she thinks of the beautiful harbour, and woe betide the one who doesn't respond positively.) Sydney Harbour is without doubt a magnificent site for a city and in recent years it has become the focus of urban life. But its vivid omnipresence has blinded Sydneysiders to the detrimental effects it has had on the city's evolution. As well as being a spectacular natural element, the harbour acts as a panacea for many urban ills. The feeling among Sydneysiders that the harbour setting alone makes Sydney 'one of the most beautiful cities in the world' provokes a laziness in design and a deficiency in the design programme which work against the city's often-expressed and deep-seated desire for cultural identity.

Sydney Harbour is the physical element that has defined the structure and determined the form of the city, and with it have come transportation, social, ecological and economic problems that have yet to be resolved.

Sydney: a guide to recent architecture

In the Central Business District (CBD), homage to the harbour has often led (particularly in the boom-time 1980s) to the subjugation of other important aspects of a building or urban design programme to the desire for a 'harbour view'. The recent focus of attention on the harbour's edge, while adding immeasurably to the city's vitality and image, has led to neglect of its traditional centre, and with most of the cultural and recreational facilities increasingly being strung like pearls around the foreshores, (particularly at Darling Harbour and Circular Quay), much of the metropolitan area is becoming disaffected. The siting of the Olympics venue is intended to go some way towards redressing this problem.

Another factor affecting architecture and urban design in Sydney is the current focus on the city's built heritage. Apart from two memorable occasions in the late 1960s and early 70s, this young city thought very little about its past until the 1980s. Having few urban traditions of its own, or building styles which hadn't been borrowed from Britain and Europe, there was little to hold back development in the boom periods of the 1960s and 70s. When in 1959 the 150-feet height limit on buildings was lifted, and controls which encouraged amalgamation of small sites and allowed floor space ratios of up to 13:1 were put into place, Sydney began its transformation to the high-rise city it is today. Total redevelopment of the then mainly Victorian and early twentieth-century city centre was envisaged by the city fathers, and, apparently, at least for the CBD, was considered by the population to be desirable.

The now historic events in which the conservation movement had its origins were the grass roots protests and the 'green bans' by the Builders' Labourers Federation on government proposals to redevelop, as high-rise commercial precincts, the historic Rocks residential area at West Circular Quay in the late 1960s, and, in the early 1970s, the old, inner-city suburb of Woolloomooloo. The protesters, who were more concerned at the time about the destruction of established low-income residential areas than the architectural heritage, were victorious, and these major triumphs for maintaining the status quo planted the seeds of the conservation movement.

In the 1980s, with the two-hundredth anniversary of European settlement approaching, Sydney began to feel the need to discern its own architectural tradition and to value its own built fabric and urban history. While developers continued to buy up sites in the CBD for ever larger, higher, free-standing towers, many architects and planners began to fear the results of wholesale demolition of the existing building stock and to abhor the lack of design quality of the many run-of-the-mill, high-rise office buildings which were appearing. By the mid 80s, the backlash against these conditions had brought about a strong conservation consciousness which began to have an impact on the changing character of the city.

While no one particularly wanted a return to a low-rise city (it was too late anyhow), Sydney sought ways to have its cake and eat it too. One of the solutions was to retain 'historic' façades and attempt to integrate high-rise buildings behind them. Another was simply to retain 'historic' buildings next to new high-rise neighbours and hope that they would reflect and fit within the context of the historic fabric. Transfer of floor space from historic building sites further increased the dichotomy between the low- and high-rise aspirations. These methods created some interesting juxtapositions of buildings, as well as some interesting contretemps between developers, their architects and the city planners. In the inner suburbs, where floor-space ratios did not increase dramatically, 'contextual design' was adopted wholeheartedly by councils. While this

Sydney: a guide to recent architecture

has helped to maintain identity and coherence for many precincts, the down-side is that it has given rise to a deadly virus of imitation nineteenth-century terraces and mock Federation (an eclectic style which emerged around the time of Australia's federation in 1901) houses, which is still attacking and spreading over the city and its suburbs at a rapid rate.

The conservation movement has saved some of Sydney's best buildings of the past, but it may also be accused of being at least partially responsible for a lack of daring and imagination in many of the city's new buildings. While there are numerous exceptions – which you will see in this book – 'heritage' and 'context' have not yet produced a dynamic urban scene in Sydney.

From its days as a convict settlement (which produced the convict architect Francis Greenway and his very fine buildings), government buildings and projects have played a large part in the development of Sydney. The Public Works Department of the State Government has produced many well-designed, significant buildings which have contributed greatly to the city's image and the coherence of its fabric, and the Government Architect, since colonial times, has been an influential figure. The Rocks and Woolloomooloo regeneration and redevelopment programmes (which resulted from the 'green bans') were both publicly funded: the former was carried out by the specially appointed Sydney Cove Authority, the latter by the Housing Department of the State Government. In the 1980s, the Darling Harbour development was carried out by the government-appointed Darling Harbour Authority. Ongoing projects include the development at Homebush Bay for the 2000 Olympics and beyond, which is being carried out by the Homebush Bay Corporation, and the regeneration of the Pyrmont Peninsula being implemented by another government authority, the City West Corporation.

The 1988 Australian Bicentenary gave a major boost to the architectural scene. State Premier Neville Wran instituted what could be described as Sydney's version of the Paris Grands Projets with the construction of Darling Harbour and the Circular Quay Promenade, the Powerhouse Museum, the Museum of Contemporary Art and many other cultural and recreational projects.

During the economic recession, present for at least five of the years represented by this book (1985–96), jobs were not available in architectural offices and the only alternative for new graduates was to set up their own practices. This is comparatively easy in Sydney. With a growing number of young professionals moving into old inner-city terraces, warehouses and apartments requiring conversion, or acquiring rugged, bushland sites (which to many would be considered unbuildable), a new school of young architects has emerged. Running small (often one-person) practices, they are designing buildings with flair, imagination and a new responsiveness to environmental conditions.

Notions of the bush and the outback have always had a powerful influence on the Australian psyche, and landscape, actual and imagined, plays a prominent part in shaping and determining building form and expression in this city. Some buildings show an inspired response to landscape and climatic conditions, while others merely adopt some of the trappings, which are now becoming as clichéd as symbols for Australian architecture as the koala and kangaroo are as symbols for the country itself.

Questions of urban design in Sydney's CBD receive a great deal of press coverage but, although the public is generally aware of, or often outraged by, some project or another, there is a noticeable lack of debate about such issues, many of which deeply affect the future of the city. Discussion tends to centre more around the civic design aspects of a project than its

Sydney: a guide to recent architecture

architectural or broader implications. The design of large city buildings is judged more by the negative impact (context, overshadowing, scale, loss of views) they may have on the environment than on any positive contributions they may make to it (expression, communication and meaning). While concerns with the former conditions are essential, it is disturbing that there is not a greater focus on innovation and the search for ways in which architecture could contribute to the shaping of the city and give expression to the creative desires and ideals of its people.

The most exciting aspect of Sydney is that it is a city still in formation. Its final shape and form have by no means been reached, nor have they yet been envisaged. Sydney is a volatile city which responds dramatically to turns and shifts in economic and market forces. In the 1980s the Sydney City Council could barely convince a developer, by either rules or gifts of bonus floor space, to build apartments in the CBD or inner suburbs. However, since the onset of the recession, when the office-building market collapsed, so many new high-rise apartments have been built, and existing high-rise office buildings, warehouses and factories converted to apartments, that it is predicted there will soon be a glut.

With the recession virtually over, with new technology rapidly reducing the tyranny of distance and a population that is becoming increasingly multicultural and urban oriented, and with the impetus of the 2000 Olympics for the city to become a showcase of architectural and urban design, the run up to the next century promises to be interesting for Sydney.

This guide shows examples from the full range of architecture to be found in Sydney – from major public and commercial buildings to small house conversions and restaurants. While the majority of the buildings discussed are in the centre, the inner suburban areas and the northern and eastern suburbs, reflecting the socio-economic conditions of the city, there are many in the western areas which are worth visiting. Several projects are included which were concerned with the organisation of public space and the making of meaningful relationships between buildings. Some interiors which are publicly accessible, and some architect-designed streetscape elements are also included.

ACKNOWLEDGEMENTS

I would like to thank all the architects whose work is included in the guide for the information they generously provided; Steve Dupont for his energetic approach to the photography; Harry Howard, Bruce Lamont, Louise Martin, Bill Morrison and Gary Porter for their interest in the project and their company on excursions to far-flung suburbs; Gabrielle Prentice for her concise comments and erudite editing; Monica Pidgeon and Elizabeth Young for their long-distance encouragement, and my father, William Morrison, for his generosity, patience and understanding throughout.

Using this book

This guide is divided into six sections which cover the various geographical areas of Sydney where there are buildings of interest. Those in the central city are best seen on foot, but public buses are fine for getting around the inner-city areas such as Paddington, Surry Hills, Newtown, Glebe, etc. It would be possible, but not very convenient, to use public transport to visit the north shore and north harbour sites, but for the western districts a car is essential. Since the streets in Sydney are relatively easy to find using a Gregory's Street Directory or UBD Guide, map coordinates have not been given.

Many of the buildings in this guide book are private residences. The owners have agreed to their houses being included on the understanding that their privacy will be respected.

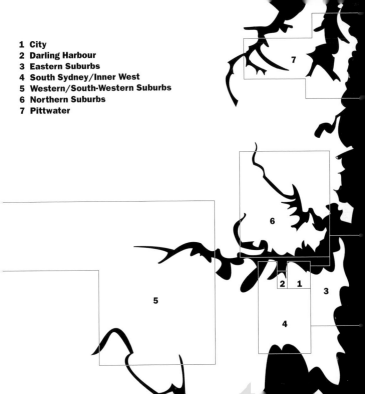

1 City
2 Darling Harbour
3 Eastern Suburbs
4 South Sydney/Inner West
5 Western/South-Western Suburbs
6 Northern Suburbs
7 Pittwater

City

Park Hyatt Hotel

Situated in the Rocks, the site of Australia's first settlement, this building was subject to stringent controls relating to height, massing and materials. The Rocks area is under the control of the Sydney Cove Authority (SCA), the State Government body set up in 1969 with a charter to plan and implement the redevelopment of the precinct in a way which retained and refurbished the general fabric of nineteenth-century workers' cottages and warehouses, and allowed sensitive, but financially rewarding, infill on particular sites. The hotel design was the result of a design/tender competition – the practice adopted by the SCA for all the major redevelopment sites. The development was also part of the Circular Quay Improvements Programme (see page 28) which created the pedestrian-movement system from Campbell's Cove to the Opera House.

The site is important as the western flank of the gateway to Circular Quay and the harbour gateway to the city. It is also directly opposite Jørn Utzon's Sydney Opera House and, from many viewpoints, closely related to the southern pylons of the Harbour Bridge. Unlike the Opera House, the hotel barely addresses the harbour. It snakes around Campbell's Cove, on which it is set, following the water's edge in a low sinuous form which allows all 200 rooms to have views across the Quay to the Opera House. For the most part, the hotel is no higher than the Dawes Point open parkland behind.

Entrance to the hotel, on the western, landward side of the building, is through a large ellipsoidal sandstone arch set in an otherwise substantially blank wall which echoes the sandstone cliff face of Dawes Point and gives insulation from the sound of Harbour Bridge traffic. The public spaces all open on to the waterfront pedestrian promenade.

The Quay façade is a well-tuned tectonic statement which relates to the scale and texture of the historic Rocks area and contrasts with the

Anchor Mortlock & Woolley 1990

City

Anchor Mortlock & Woolley 1990

stark, engineered monumentality of the approaches to the Harbour Bridge. Its framework is a rhythmic pattern of repeated double bays within which window and balcony variations take place and the division of the façade into base, body and roof-level loggias is articulated. However, the two small roof towers (which contain plant) are purely context-pastiche and are peculiarly and disappointingly out of sync with the otherwise intricately modulated expression of the building. Colours and materials also pay deference to those of the Rocks.

In all, this is a successful building, performing its urban duties well, but one wonders whether a little dash of rebellion, an innovative breaking of the rules, say, in the use of materials, or a more imaginative solution to the roofscape, might not have given it an extra magic of its own.

ADDRESS 7 Hickson Road, the Rocks
STRUCTURAL ENGINEER Ove Arup & Partners
LANDSCAPE ARCHITECT Conybeare Morrison & Partners
CLIENT CRI Limited for EIE Australia
SIZE 18,168 square metres COST AUD$45 million
ACCESS public

City

Anchor Mortlock & Woolley 1990

Anchor Mortlock & Woolley 1990

Rocks Square

The site, in the heart of the Rocks, includes the only open space in the precinct which can be described as a square. As it is also one of the few purely pedestrian spaces in the area it is a natural focus for tourist and retail activities. The design programme called for a major new shopping centre, sympathetic to the historic area, to be created from the refurbishment of a heritage-protected 1918 industrial building and an adjoining, very basic, 1970s residential and commercial building. Also, the square was to be upgraded and covered public space provided.

The architects adopted a palimpsest approach, layering new construction over old so as to allow much of the original structure to stay in place. Fronting the rebuilt and enlarged Rocks Square is a double-height arcade formed simply by the erection of a new brick wall. Separated from the original 1970s building by a butterfly-shaped glazed roof which gently confounds the eye with its arched internal layer of sunscreening, the arcade provides a transition space between square and shopping centre which, defined by light and the play of shadows on softly coloured brickwork, has transformed Rocks Square from simplistic spatial relationships to a subtle complexity of interrelated, flowing spaces.

The internal levels of the 1970s building were reconstructed, and the massive new brick façades kept clearly separate from the original structure. This is a building which, in the words of the architects, 'declines to obliterate the past'. Yet it is undeniably of its own time.

ADDRESS Argyle and Playfair Streets, the Rocks
CLIENT Sydney Cove Authority
STRUCTURAL ENGINEER Paterson Wholohan Grill
SITE AREA 1,940 square metres COST AUD\$5 million
ACCESS public

City

Tonkin Zulaikha Harford 1994

Tonkin Zulaikha Harford 1994

Immigration House

The Sydney Cove Authority brief was for a substantial building to be integrated into the narrow street pattern on a site at the top of the Rocks near the approaches to the Harbour Bridge. As usual for this area, the brief had a considerable effect on the form and expression of the development. The site was subject to a six-storey building envelope, and to controls requiring façades of face or rendered brickwork, windows compatible in scale and rhythm to those of surrounding buildings, and a glass area no greater than 50 per cent. A retail street was to have been created with additions to the Argyle Bond Store directly opposite, opening it on to Gloucester Walk, but neither this nor a pedestrian link through the building, from the waterfront to the Harbour Bridge, has been realised. As a result, the building has been left somewhat stranded, not easily accessible from the more lively, lower areas of the Rocks, and unable to support the envisaged mix of uses.

Within the constraints, this is a sophisticated solution, but it breaks no new ground. Its streamlined horizontal massing is accentuated by strong divisions into base, centre and top, and is modulated by the careful arrangement and detailing of brickwork, fenestration, balconies and balustrades. Two sides of the almost triangular building meet in a circular tower on the northern end. The eastern façade is punctuated by the three-storey-high opening for the originally proposed pedestrian link.

ADDRESS 88 Cumberland Street, the Rocks
CLIENT Sydney Cove Redevelopment Authority, now the Sydney Cove Authority
STRUCTURAL ENGINEER Partridge Partners Pty Ltd
SIZE 7,400 square metres COST AUD$8 million
ACCESS public areas

City

Daryl Jackson Robin Dyke Pty Ltd/Baker Associates Architects 1991

Sailors Thai

Sailors Thai restaurant, named after the historic Sailors' Home that it occupies, is related to Darley St Thai in Kings Cross – both have the same proprietor and designer, Iain Halliday. It offers two different styles of eating in two distinct areas. Although there is internal access between them, the noodle bar, noisy and busy, has its main entry on George Street, and the split-level dining room, more enclosed and tranquil, is entered through the bar area, from the side passageway which leads down to the waterfront.

The design is cool, serene and minimalist, with objects of definitive geometric form (like the waiters' station, an aluminium-clad cylinder) contrasting with the rough textures of the sandstone building. In the main dining room, the potential starkness is softened by the fresh pastel colours of the smooth stucco panels which stand out from the sandstone back-drop like vibrant, wall-size paintings. A pale concrete floor connects the dining rooms and the bar area, where concrete and glass blocks are massed to form the bar itself, the only object in the space.

The striking design feature of the long narrow noodle bar is the aluminium dining bench which runs from front to back down the centre of the space, seating approximately 15 people on each side. An open aluminium kitchen runs the length of the restaurant along one wall. Walls are a nutty brown and the original timber floor has been retained.

Sailors Thai exhibits an order that is relaxed and a sparseness that is friendly.

ADDRESS 106 George Street, the Rocks
CLIENT David Thompson and Peter Bower
SIZE 260 square metres COST AUD$300,000
ACCESS open

Burley Katon Halliday 1995

Burley Katon Halliday 1995

Circular Quay Promenade

Circular Quay is the harbour gateway to Sydney, but before improvements were implemented (as a Bicentennial Project) its foreshore was largely alienated from public use. Although the Opera House and the Rocks attracted several million visitors a year, Circular Quay, with its dilapidated wharves and surface car-parking occupying invaluable waterside land, was used for little more than a transport interchange, albeit one through which tens of thousands of commuters passed every day. The approach to the Opera House featured a temporary, ugly covered way, and its forecourt was a staff parking lot. A public road ran between the Maritime Services Board Building (now the Museum of Contemporary Art) and the area between the southern end of the Overseas Passenger Terminal and Campbell's Cove, giving no access to pedestrians. Circular Quay Railway Station obscured the view from the city to the harbour.

The potential for the creation of a pedestrian promenade from the Opera House to the Harbour Bridge was recognised by the City Council in its 1971 Strategic Plan, but most of the land and buildings involved were owned by a multitude of State Government bodies and the Council was unable to act on its proposals.

After an Ideas Competition held by the RAIA and an international architectural conference in Sydney in 1983, at which participants such as Kenneth Frampton, Jaqueline Robertson and Helmut Jahn publicly criticised the lack of appropriate design for this highly significant area, the State Government was virtually shamed into taking a decision to act. A Steering Committee of representatives of all the government bodies was appointed. The development reports it produced were the result of a remarkable exercise in co-operation between bodies which had previously taken decisions entirely autonomously with little thought for the impact they might have on the wider urban scene. At the end of 1984

Various 1988

the Public Works Department was appointed the construction authority, and a team of architects and urban designers from several private practices, plus the Government Architects branch, proceeded with design development and documentation.

Through a series of interventions – the closure and rationalisation of roads to form parks and promenades, the truncation of the Overseas Passenger Terminal to provide space for a waterfront square, the remodelling of the railway station and the ferry wharves to allow views to the harbour, the removal of crumbling wharf structures and the creation of new levels of access to the harbour's edge and the approach to the Opera House, the replanning of bus routes and their termini, the co-ordination of landscaping, paving, lighting and street furniture throughout, and the orchestration of all restaurant and retailing activity – Circular Quay was transformed into the vibrant public place it is today.

There have been calls for many years for the Cahill Expressway (the elevated roadway which runs along the southern edge of Circular Quay above the railway line) to be pulled down; no doubt it will eventually go, but not before 2000. However, another recent Ideas Competition (for the creation of a large public square at central Circular Quay) has produced some exciting designs which may realise results in the next few years.

ADDRESS Circular Quay from the Harbour Bridge to the Opera House
CLIENT NSW Government
ARCHITECTS NSW Government Architect; Allen Jack + Cottier;
Conybeare Morrison & Partners; Lawrence Nield & Partners
STRUCTURAL ENGINEER Wholohan & Grill
LENGTH 2 kilometres COST AUD$100 million
ACCESS public

City

Various 1988

Various 1988

Overseas Passenger Terminal

Prior to 1988 the Overseas Passenger Terminal was one of the ugliest, most obtrusive buildings on Circular Quay. It was a 1950s flat-topped slab building with no redeeming features other than the bright 50s colours of the laminated plastic panels on its façades. It was definitely best viewed when obscured by a passenger liner and, although it had been the venue for many jolly overseas farewells, its sudden transformation into one of the most exciting and eloquent buildings in the Circular Quay panorama prompted no nostalgic protests.

As part of the Circular Quay Improvements Programme the architects were commissioned in 1984 to investigate how to shorten the under-used terminal building to free up more of the precious waterfront area for public space. When the heavy cladding was removed a light, elegant, steel structure was revealed, and this, unadorned, was used as the basis of the new design.

The impact of the existing elevated road which ran along its western façade, with ramped access and egress at either end, was diminished by replacing the ramp at the southern end with an elevated roundabout. This also allowed the southern third of the building to be removed for the formation of a large waterfront square and a new park, and opened up views from George Street across to the Opera House.

The Passenger Terminal remains a working structure: cruise liners still berth there and there are cargo and customs facilities, a baggage hall and associated maritime amenities. Now the building itself is as exciting as any cruise ship. It is a dynamic sculpture of rust-coloured steel and glass elements – canopies, turrets, towers, balconies and platforms, escalators, stairways and ramps – all sliding under or over, projecting horizontally or emerging vertically from the original steel skeleton. At night its structure is defined by a blaze of light.

Lawrence Nield & Partners 1988

Lawrence Nield & Partners 1988

There is a first-class restaurant with superb views in the glass tower at the northern end, a restaurant and café at ground-floor level opening on to major public spaces, and public viewing platforms on upper-level walkways. When no ship is berthed, the eastern wharf apron becomes part of the public Circular Quay promenade.

ADDRESS Circular Quay West
ASSOCIATED ARCHITECT NSW Government Architect
STRUCTURAL ENGINEER Ove Arup & Partners
SIZE 7,000 square metres COST AUD$16 million
ACCESS public areas

Lawrence Nield & Partners 1988

City

City

Lawrence Nield & Partners 1988

Museum of Contemporary Art

A prominent building, which was always a rather too imposing reminder of inflexible bureaucracy and reams of red-tape to be loved by Sydney-siders, has undergone an extraordinary transformation into a lively, symbolically open cultural centre which interacts easily with its surroundings. In 1962 Sydney University received a £2-million bequest from the medical doctor, artist and collector John Wardell Power, to found a centre for the study and development of modern art. The collection of avant-garde works he started was initially shown in a small gallery at the university. There were insufficient funds for the establishment of a museum until the NSW Government provided the 1939 Maritime Services Board Headquarters Building at Circular Quay West on a 50-year lease at the nominal rent of $500 per year.

The six-storey building had a large floor plate and stood alone on an ideal site facing the Opera House between the Circular Quay Promenade and George Street. But it was far from ideal for exhibiting modern works of art. Its ceilings were low, its spaces cramped, with few naturally ventilated and daylit areas. It was considered also to be a building too monumental to attract the passing crowd.

Given the budget constraints, the architectural decision was to allow, as far as possible, the main features of the existing building – stairs, levels and, in many instances, decoration and detail – to be integrated into the new environment, with the maximum amount of space given to the galleries. This has resulted in some crowding and confusion around the foyer, but this is a people's palace of art and it doesn't really seem to matter. To create the sequence of rectangular galleries, gypsum plank shells, some with gently vaulted ceilings, were placed inside the existing skeleton and skin. These shells splay back at the corners revealing windows which provide softly reflected light and spectacular harbour views.

Peddle Thorp Architects 1993

City

To give the MCA a friendlier face on George Street, a new two-storey front, sandstone-dressed to relate to both the museum building and the surrounding Rocks buildings, was built to the street line. Its two distinct blocks, each roofed with a copper barrel vault, stand on either side of the central entrance, which is differentiated further by a small sculpture terrace on its roof. This addition contains revenue-producing outlets (including the MCA shop), extensions to the first-floor galleries, and access through to the main Circular Quay entry foyer. This foyer, and the first gallery one enters, are the only sections of the building where structural alterations have taken place. A floor has been removed to create the double-storey-height space (and allow access through the building from street to waterfront) and a double-height gallery which interacts spatially with the galleries above.

The MCA forecourt, which is regularly used for the display of large temporary sculptures, faces the Quay (as does the terrace of the museum's restaurant). With no walls, fences or other obstructions between the forecourt, the public garden beyond and the waterfront promenade, a natural interplay of activity occurs between all these areas.

ADDRESS 140 George Street, Circular Quay West
CLIENT Museum of Contemporary Art
STRUCTURAL ENGINEER George Clarke, Knox & Associates
COST AUD$12 million
ACCESS every day 11.00–18.00

City

Peddle Thorp Architects 1993

City

Peddle Thorp Architects 1993

Bennnelong Restaurant, Sydney Opera House

In its previous incarnation the Bennelong Restaurant could have been in any building anywhere. Red plush carpet covered its floor and walls; tall, bronze tree-branch lamps were dotted throughout; red-lacquered planter boxes were filled with palm trees, and a large bar displaying a lot of brass and glass was a prominent feature. The design of the restaurant totally ignored the fact that it was situated in one of the most remarkable buildings in the world, and on an extraordinary site with a spectacular panoramic backdrop of city buildings and wing-side scenery of Sydney Harbour. All the decorative glitz, the bar, the square platform (which projected from the upper level bearing a baby grand piano) and the net curtains which hung over much of the glazing, made it very difficult to appreciate the intrinsic qualities of the awe-inspiring, multi-level space contained under the two small shell roofs designed by Jørn Utzon.

When the Bennelong was taken over by Gay Bilson, one of Australia's leading restaurateurs (her previous restaurant, Berowra Waters Inn, was designed by Glenn Murcutt), Leigh Prentice's first response was 'to clear out all the rubbish and let the space and the shells speak for themselves'. Letting the building speak for itself became the strategy for the whole design.

An early sketch plan by Utzon shows an open, multi-layered space with an *à la carte* restaurant in the lower level and a supper club/grill at the top. The requirements of Gay Bilson's brief for the new Bennelong were remarkably similar – an *à la carte* dining area, a more relaxed supper area and a cocktail bar.

When it was stripped, the space regained its sense of balance. Views were opened up, and the granite-surfaced steps (part of the grand external staircase leading to the performance halls) and the granite floors and walls

Leigh Prentice & Associates 1995

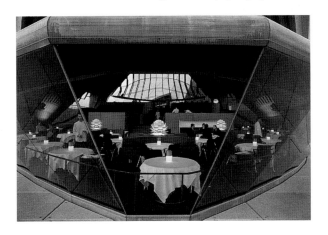

City

Leigh Prentice & Associates 1995

of the central podium were revealed. Now the space conveyed the sense of shells poised on a podium, and the internal spatial qualities and the relationship with the outside were re-established. The critical design problem was how to create a restaurant which would give diners a sense of intimacy without denying the newly revealed spatial relationships. This has been achieved with a minimum of additional work.

Entrance to the restaurant is from the Opera House foyer (situated under the podium) and up a narrow flight of steps which emerge on the central level from where the two intersecting shells rise. In the new Bennelong this level is left with its granite floor to become the bar/lounge. The bar itself (much reduced in size from its predecessor) fits with smooth, clean lines into the corner of the podium opposite the entry, and nothing here rises above the level of the podium walls. White Arne Jacobsen swan chairs sit on the circle of electric-blue carpet that delineates the cocktail lounge, which has been dubbed 'Swan Lake' by the clientele.

To differentiate between the structure and the insertions, a language of circular shapes and cylindrical forms was developed. Three multi-faceted seating booths on the lower floor organise the use of the space in such a way that intimacy and privacy are achieved and spatial flow maintained. The only elements which rise above booth height are the three Fritz Hansen artichoke lights at the centre of each booth. From the top level a large circular booth with five tables within its circumference projects out to become a cylinder reaching down the steps. It gives structure to the space and dramatic crow's-nest views over the bar and lower level. The rest of the seating on both floors is at individual circular tables.

The other significant consideration in the design of the new Bennelong was the lighting. The basic scheme for lighting the shells throughout the Opera House is a system of low-level uplights emanating from the point

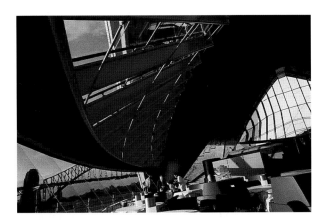

City

Leigh Prentice & Associates 1995

where the ribs gather. These create a layered effect, illuminating the ceilings and throwing the ribs into silhouette. Although this was not sufficient for the total lighting of the restaurant, the architect decided to build on the chiaroscuro effect. By placing floodlights in the upper reaches of the shells an adequate low level of ambient lighting was achieved throughout the space. The use of simple white-glass battery-run table lamps which light diners' faces, leaving their bodies and surroundings in the dark, creates pools of light which complement the dramatic effect of the ribs.

The other insertion in the space was a new boxed-in service area adjacent to the entry stairs and leading to the kitchen.

With these simple but carefully considered, well-designed and detailed interventions (not to mention the reputation of the food), the Bennelong has become a restaurant worthy of the superb building it inhabits.

ADDRESS Sydney Opera House
CLIENT Gardner Merchant Australia
SIZE 725 square metres
COST AUD$1.1 million
ACCESS open evenings only

City

Leigh Prentice & Associates 1995

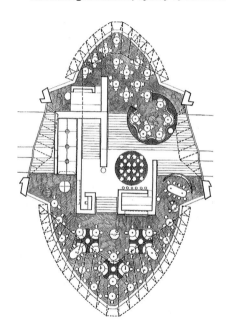

City

Leigh Prentice & Associates 1995

Wharf Theatre

The Sydney Theatre Company and the Sydney Dance Company occupy this 1914 finger-wharf warehouse, one of five such heavy timber structures which project from Hickson Road over 200 metres into Walsh Bay, just west of the Harbour Bridge. The building was converted originally for the theatre company. Its enormous size allowed the entire operation – a 350-seat live theatre, dressing rooms, three large rehearsal rooms, workshops and storage rooms, plus green room, foyer, bar and restaurant – to be accommodated on the first floor, leaving the entire ground floor of the pier unoccupied. In 1987 half this floor was converted for all the requirements, except performance space, of the dance company.

The public spaces of the building are at the end of the pier, taking advantage of the 180-degree harbour views. Entry, up stairs to the first floor, then along a wide gallery which runs the full 230-metre length of the building on the eastern side, is an exciting and educational experience. As well as the rhythmic framing of tantalising views, there is an opportunity to study the original, massive iron-bark structure and the panoply of posters of past performances. And, as one takes advantage of the access to the mezzanine-level gallery along the western side, the internal workings of the theatre can be observed also.

Externally the building has been little altered, except at the northern foyer/restaurant end which is totally glazed with two open decks occupying the corners.

ADDRESS Piers 4 and 5, Hickson Road, Walsh Bay
ASSOCIATED ARCHITECT NSW Government Architect
STRUCTURAL ENGINEER Ove Arup & Partners
SIZE 8,600 square metres COST AUD$3.7 million
ACCESS Monday to Saturday 9.00–21.00

Vivian Fraser Architect 1986

City

Vivian Fraser Architect 1986

Grosvenor Place

Harry Seidler had to forgo his plans for an open plaza on the south-east corner of this site when the Sydney Cove Authority insisted that he retain the façades and part of the fabric of two Edwardian buildings. The plaza would have allowed an unobstructed view of the full length of this elegant tower from the southern approach and much freer movement around the site. Seidler accused the Heritage Council and the Authority of 'façadism', seeing the situation as an example of the city's unpreparedness to grasp new opportunities and design and build for the future. It was a highly publicised issue at the time and Sydney still talks about the pros and cons of the decision.

Grosvenor Place is located at the northern end of the Central Business District, maximising north-eastern harbour views by taking the form of two opposing quadrants which slip slightly away from each other to allow fire stairs in the gap at each end. The main approach to the building – at the northern corner where two small circular towers form a gateway into the partially enclosed, granite-paved, gently rising forecourt – has the rigorous appeal of the pure modernist aesthetic. The 46-storey tower is straight ahead, filling up the field of vision with its splendid curving façade, which has a strong geometry made dynamic by the varying angles of aluminium sun louvres. The enticing cool-grey granite recesses of the soaring lobby are given a touch of colour by three large Frank Stella relief paintings on the walls between the lift banks.

The plan form of Grosvenor Place, based on a precise geometry, and the use of steel for the structure, allowed a long-span, column-free system of construction in which all the structural spans, and therefore the beams and façade elements, are identical.

The floors are 14.6 metres deep, rentable office space totals 90,000 square metres, and typical floor areas contain up to 2,000 square metres

Harry Seidler & Associates/Davis, Heather & Dysart 1988

City

Harry Seidler & Associates/Davis, Heather & Dysart 1988

of open, flexible floor space. The external columns of the tower are gathered together in groups of three with v-shaped transfer members to form circular caissons.

The tower occupies just over one quarter of the site, allowing space on its south-western side for a glass-roofed outdoor café plaza adjacent to the old restored buildings.

ADDRESS corner of Grosvenor and George Streets
CLIENT Grosvenor Place Pty Ltd
STRUCTURAL ENGINEER Ove Arup & Partners
SIZE 102,000 square metres COST AUD$180 million
ACCESS public areas

Harry Seidler & Associates/Davis, Heather & Dysart 1988

City

Harry Seidler & Associates/Davis, Heather & Dysart 1988

Macquarie Street Boulevard

Macquarie Street, Sydney's major boulevard, is redolent with the city's past. Linking Hyde Park to the Opera House, it runs north–south along the ridge that defines the eastern edge of the city, through a panoply of its architectural history. The eastern side of the street is lined with some of the city's grandest public buildings, and the western side features office buildings from practically every decade since 1880. For the Bicentenary various building programmes were carried out which were intended to establish the grandeur that was inherent in the street's nature but had never been fully realised. These included, in addition to streetscape works, the conversion of the Hyde Park Barracks and the Government Mint into museums, the restoration of the State Parliament buildings, plans for a new State Library building, and restoration of the Sydney Hospital.

Before the streetscape works were implemented, Macquarie Street could hardly have been described as a boulevard. With few trees, narrow footpaths and traffic congestion, it offered little incentive to stroll or linger. The boulevard landscape was created by planting mature plane trees the full length of the street. Footpaths were doubled in width, paved with brick and granite, and set up with cafés and kiosks. Features include the plaza treatment of Queens Square at the Hyde Park end and the redesigned forecourt at the Palace Gates entrance to the Gardens.

The street furniture designed by the architects for this project was later used in various other city precincts, and the slatted timber seat has been copied and produced by manufacturers all over Sydney.

ADDRESS Macquarie Street
CLIENT NSW Public Works Department
STRUCTURAL ENGINEER Acer Wargon Chapman
COST AUD$16 million

City

Conybeare Morrison & Partners/NSW Government Architect 1988

State Library of New South Wales

This glassy new library (a Bicentenary project) is an addition to the existing neoclassical sandstone building designed in 1907 by the Colonial Architect, Walter Liberty Vernon, and built progressively up until 1960. The main requirements of the design programme were that the library should reveal itself to the passer-by like a shopfront, be user-friendly (no daunting grandiose steps in the manner of the entrance to the early building), be open and flexible internally, and respect the historic buildings of Macquarie Street.

Great care has gone into the design of the building to achieve these objectives (seven of its floors are underground to maintain scale), but there is some doubt as to whether they have given rise to the best solution. While the new building, with its rhythms, colours and cadences taking their cues from the context, is a respectable addition to the street, the cacophony of sounds resonating in the General Reference Library (including the sound of footsteps on the Wombeyan marble foyer floor) leaves one longing for the peace, tranquillity and visual order of the wonderful, top-lit Reading Room of the old building.

The 'vivid succession of spaces, sudden changes of level, voids going through two or more floors, dramatic views into the street' do 'make it a rich architectural experience', as the architect says, but perhaps one too rich and exciting for the purpose of the building. Great, if you don't have to do serious work there.

ADDRESS Macquarie Street
CLIENT State Library of New South Wales
STRUCTURAL ENGINEER Taylor Thomson Whitting
SIZE 22,525 square metres COST AUD$33 million
ACCESS open every day

City

NSW Government Architect 1992

City

NSW Government Architect 1992

Parliament House

This extension to the State Parliament House was the first of the recent additions to be erected in Sydney's historic Macquarie Street. Commenced in pre-postmodernist 1974, it is a successful example of a strictly modernist intervention in a heritage environment.

Built on a large site adjacent to the southern end of the State Library, between the existing Parliament buildings and the grassy slopes of the Domain, the building provides accommodation for members and staff, a library, meeting rooms, bars, dining and recreational facilities, and parking. It is companion to an ensemble of two-storey buildings – the 1811 Rum Hospital (the central building), the 1843 Legislative Assembly Chamber to its north, and the 1856 'temporary' Legislative Council (a prefabricated cast-iron building sent from England to Melbourne for use on the Victorian goldfields) – which are diminutive in comparison.

The extension was designed so as not to be seen from Macquarie Street (five of its 12 floors are below ground) and to create a strong urban edge to Hospital Road at the rear. While the fenestration pattern is definitely Corbusian, the colours of the precast panelling suggest the hue of the sandstone State Library, and the column spacing consciously echoes that of the portico of the old Rum Hospital. Its location allowed a site for the library extension, a new public space and a route from Macquarie Street to the Domain. Entry is from the Macquarie Street buildings through a large top-lit central space with a fountain by Robert Woodward.

ADDRESS Macquarie Street
CLIENT NSW Government
STRUCTURAL ENGINEER Taylor Thomson Whitting
COST AUD$65 million
ACCESS public areas, weekdays 9.30–16.00

City

NSW Government Architect 1985

NSW Government Architect 1985

Hyde Park Barracks Museum

Designed by the convict Government Architect, Francis Greenway, the Hyde Park Barracks (1817) and the St James Church opposite form a significant Georgian townscape ensemble at the top of Macquarie Street. Originally built to provide quarters for 1,400 convicts, the Barracks also accommodated many other groups, including Irish immigrants, distressed needlewomen, the infirm and the insane. For most of this century the building housed District Courts, until it was restored and refurbished as a museum of social history in 1984. In 1990 the building was placed in the hands of the Historic Houses Trust to establish a museum of its own history.

The Government Architect's restoration of the Barracks revealed to Sydney the exquisite treasure that the building is, and confirmed its place in the architectural and urban history of the city. The conversion of the building to a museum dedicated to its own history opened up another source of riches, a new depth of history and an exciting, palpable way of looking at the past.

The programme called for the rationalisation of the building's services and the removal of additions that concealed its fabric and fascinating history. It required systems that could touch the building but in no way cause further damage. Any intervention undertaken in the 1990s was to be clearly distinguishable from the surviving fabric and the interventions of the 1980s.

All new work had to be reversible, which led to the fundamental design parameter that each new element would touch the building lightly. To achieve this a language of steel, aluminium and glass was developed.

The architects have presented the building as layers of history, revealing aspects of its fabric and secrets of its past in a manner which brings them into the present with a haunting reality. One feature, the ghost stair,

Tonkin Zulaikha Harford 1991

Tonkin Zulaikha Harford 1991

is a steel suspended outline structure that traces the handrail of the original stairs up through the three levels of the museum.

In every way this building is a gem. From the tactile, auditory, crunchy experience of entering through the pebble-covered courtyard, to the surrealistic yet simple and eerie experience of the shadow figures on the walls of one of the rooms, the building speaks to you – not only of its own history, but of an excellent collaboration between the architects and the museum.

ADDRESS Queens Square, Macquarie Street
CLIENT Historic Houses Trust of New South Wales
ARCHITECT (1984 renovation) NSW Government Architect
STRUCTURAL ENGINEER McBean & Crisp
SIZE 1,500 square metres
COST AUD$1.5 million (museum interior and fitout)
ACCESS open every day

City

Tonkin Zulaikha Harford 1991

City

Tonkin Zulaikha Harford 1991

Sydney Hospital & Sydney Eye Hospital

This project involved the relocation of the Eye Hospital to the campus of the historic Sydney Hospital site on Macquarie Street. Since the restored 1890s hospital buildings close the Martin Place vista and constitute important elements in the urban streetscape, heritage issues were thoroughly discussed before a final design was agreed on for the new four-storey building, which sits on six levels of underground public parking.

The principles that shaped the design relate to the formal geometry, spatial hierarchies, scale, architectural themes and details of the existing complex of buildings. The building's siting reinforces existing courtyard spaces, its base is lined in sandstone to match the historic buildings, and the car-park lift shaft relates to the turrets on the centre block. Special attention was given to the echoing of solid to void, flat and relief surfaces, shaded verandah themes, and vertical and horizontal rhythms. Light metalwork and solid stone elements were used to preserve and enhance the ambience of the site.

All this attention to context results in a good building with many visual rewards, but after a trip along Macquarie Street one longs for something modern that not only relates but is also a piece of dazzling design in its own right.

ADDRESS Macquarie Street
CLIENT NSW Government
ARCHITECTS NSW Government Architect, Fletcher Constructions, McConnell Smith & Johnson
STRUCTURAL ENGINEER Building Structures Design Group
SIZE 7,000 square metres plus 1,000 square metres car park
COST AUD$22 million
ACCESS public areas

City

Various 1995

City

Various 1995

The Art Gallery of New South Wales has been evolving since architect John Horbury Hunt designed a stark, windowless, temporary building of bare brick on the site in the Domain in 1885. The imposing neoclassical façade and southern picture galleries were added in 1897, to a plan by Colonial Architect, Walter Liberty Vernon, which was intended to replace the temporary gallery. In 1899, 1901 and 1902 further galleries, the grand oval lobby and the portico were completed to his design. In 1972 the remaining parts of the Hunt building were demolished and the new Captain Cook Wing was completed by architect Andrew Andersons to Vernon's original footprint, complementing the early work with its plain sandstone façades. The new wing doubled the exhibition space and provided an additional temporary gallery and a restaurant.

The latest additions, by the same architect, were built as a Bicentennial project to the east of the existing structure, and once again doubled the gallery's size. This wing expanded the display space for the permanent collections, including new galleries for Aboriginal art, Asian art, prints, drawings and photography, and added a 350-seat theatre, a café, and a rooftop sculpture garden and terrace. This new four-storey addition has a low, stepped profile and is clad in Sydney sandstone to minimise physical intrusion into the Domain, the expanse of parkland to the east of Macquarie Street. The post-tensioned reinforced-concrete roof beams repeat the vocabulary of the Captain Cook Wing, and the generous use of natural lighting enhances the form and clarity of the internal spaces. They flow easily from new to old and between different levels.

In this building it is possible to contemplate the art in an appropriately pure and calm environment, without ever suffering from the pressure of museum claustrophobia. And every so often there is a breathtaking view of the harbour, a glimpse of Woolloomooloo or a refreshing sight of the

NSW Government Architect 1988

City

NSW Government Architect 1988

verdant slopes of the Domain, which make you aware that art, after all, is derived from life and landscape.

Because of its significance in the hierarchy of building types, the Art Gallery has had an influence on Sydney architecture which has been not altogether liberating. Although the building's extension into the landscape is tight and controlled, it doesn't break any rules or create any new dialogues. Its incredibly good manners can be somewhat stultifying.

ADDRESS Art Gallery Road
CLIENT NSW Government
STRUCTURAL ENGINEER Taylor Thomson Whitting
SIZE 11,000 square metres COST AUD$25 million
ACCESS Monday to Saturday 10.00–17.00, Sunday 11.00–17.00

City

NSW Government Architect 1988

NSW Government Architect 1988

Royal Botanic Gardens Glasshouses

The function of a glasshouse in the Sydney climate is quite different from that of its European counterpart. It is more concerned with provision of the appropriate light, humidity and ventilation for healthy growth and protection against excessive sunlight, heat and dry winds than with protection against cold. However, these differences in function do not necessarily mean differences in form.

The existing glasshouse's dramatic pyramid form was unsuitable for a range of plant material. A new linear building was needed, more in the style of a traditional, vaulted glasshouse, with a cross-section resembling the shape of a large tree canopy extending out to an adjoining lower space.

The establishment of a relationship between a new, long, vaulted building and the existing pyramid was a critical aspect of the design programme, for which the architect produced a sophisticated geometric solution. A circular vault curving around the arc of a quadrant centres on the existing pyramid, relating to its four-sided symmetry and diagonals. Its fluid forms soften the pyramid's stark formalism yet at the same time bring it into a sharper focus. A sloping glass plane, at the same angle as the pyramid, carries the vaulted form to the ground while, on the uphill side, a blank retaining wall acts as a backdrop to a series of internal terraces which enable visitors to inspect the plants, full-grown trees, palms and ferns from various levels. An artificial stream traverses the building and emerges to form a pool between the old and new glasshouses.

ADDRESS Mrs Macquarie's Road, Royal Botanic Gardens
CLIENT Royal Botanic Gardens
STRUCTURAL ENGINEER James Taylor & Associates
SIZE 600 square metres COST AUD$3 million
ACCESS every day 10.00–16.00

Anchor Mortlock & Woolley 1993

Anchor Mortlock & Woolley 1993

Governor Phillip and Governor Macquarie Towers, Museum of Sydney and First Government House Plaza

The recent history of the site of Australia's first Government House is almost as interesting as its past. Incredibly, the site, on the corner of Bridge and Phillip Streets, had stood empty for 50 years, adorned only by a tin shed and the hundreds of motorcycles that parked there every day. In this prestigious area of Sydney – the hub of the financial district and rich with illustrious sandstone buildings and redolent with colonial history – an empty site was an anomaly. But this one had been vacant for so long the Sydney citizenry didn't really notice; and the developers, who were having a fine time knocking down a large number of Victorian buildings, had no use for it until all those possibilities were exhausted. It was known that the site of the first government building was in the vicinity, but until the 1980s nobody thought much about it. However, in the late 1970s and early 1980s several things happened to change the situation: architecture and planning professionals became more aware of urban design considerations and made constant criticisms of the empty corner site, which detracted from the civic qualities of Bridge Street; the government decided it wanted to realise some returns on its site; and the nation developed a desire to discover its own history.

There was a development proposal in 1982 for a high-rise commercial building, but an earlier archaeological investigation had revealed parts of the brick footings of First Government House. With the city's new-found historical awareness, the idea of a high-rise building sitting on top of the fragile remains of the country's European birthplace was not popular, even if the structure would avoid damaging the remains and the ground floor was given over to a museum. That proposal did not go

Denton Corker Marshall 1994

Denton Corker Marshall 1994

ahead, but the government found a solution by transferring floor space rights from the by now hallowed site to another one immediately behind. This was owned by developer Sid Londish, who masterminded the amalgamation of the whole area, making development feasible.

The final site covered the whole block between Bridge, Phillip, Bent and Young Streets. The design programme required the conservation of the remains of First Government House *in situ*, the provision of a commemorative display and museum, the preservation and restoration of the existing historic terraces, and the building of a commercially viable office development. As built, the development comprises five related elements – Governor Phillip Tower, Governor Macquarie Tower, First Government House Plaza, the Museum of Sydney, and two rows of historic terrace houses converted to boutique office space.

Governor Phillip Tower dominates the site. The razor-sharp, steel blades of the egg-crate top of this 64-level, ice-cool block of granite and glass cut into the sky higher than any other building in the city. However, the view of the Governor Phillip from street level, with its visually over-riding expression of the repetition of massive, zinc-covered transfer beams, is not so attractive. These beams lift the tower ten floors off the ground, giving it grandiosely high foyers and, with the resulting unob-structed harbour views, equally high floor space rentals.

The 39-level Governor Macquarie Tower adjoins the Governor Phillip on its southern side. Although clad in the same expensive materials and detailed with the same care and attention, the Governor Macquarie does appear rather as a squat little brother. Having no dramatic headdress, and with its feet firmly planted on the ground, the relationship between the two high-rise buildings, despite the four-storey sandstone base which successfully unites most of the elements of the site, is awkward and unsat-

Denton Corker Marshall 1994

City

Denton Corker Marshall 1994

isfying. Entry to these two buildings is from Farrer Place into the high gallery space which runs between them and links through to Phillip Street. The foyers are so impressive in scale, materials and detailing that they are almost oppressive.

At the Bridge Street end of the development is First Government House Plaza. It is the open-air portion of the Museum of Sydney and an important addition to the city's public spaces. The museum and the plaza are the resounding successes of the whole scheme and, in so far as their presence and integrity are established and maintained within the context of the predominance of the adjacent 64-storey building (from the base of which the tiny museum obtrudes), that aspect of the development must be judged successful.

The plaza, designed with a controlled and confident minimalism, interprets and recalls many of the site's past activities and subtly evokes a sense of its history. Although the plaza covers most of the remaining footings of the historic structure, any of the new paving elements can be removed and the fragments viewed through a glass pyramid which fits over their 2-metre-square grid. The outline of the original footings is marked on the paving through a change of texture and materials and can be viewed from the museum above. The projecting, symbolic, sandstone museum wall, forming the backdrop to the plaza, is partially built from materials recovered during the on-site archaeological dig. The museum itself is a sleek, elegant slither of steel-framed and glass units, organised between this wall and another vast sandstone wall which is part of the base of Governor Phillip Tower. The museum's contemporary design language is a major vehicle in enabling the site's histories to be expressed. From an urban design perspective, it is extremely disappointing that there are no routes through the development from the museum to the office buildings.

Denton Corker Marshall 1994

With this development, Sydney has entered a new era of state-of-the-art architecture, albeit commercial. This is no cheapo, slapstick developer job. Nor is it post-modern New York deco pastiche. Its roots are in modernism; it delves deeply into current architectural theory and it is certainly one of the most interesting and important building developments that Sydney has seen, lifting the game to new levels as far as materials and detailing go and adding a great deal of intellectual content and game-playing. But that is not to say it is entirely successful. No matter what symbolism may have been attributed to the enormous vacant spaces between tower and base, they stem from a commercial rather than an intellectual or design imperative, and their thrusting, compressive strength symbolises, more than anything else, the supremacy of pragmatic commercial considerations over other factors in the design of the city.

ADDRESS Phillip, Bridge, Young, Bent Streets
CLIENTS State Superannuation Authority, Comrealty, Historic Houses Trust
STRUCTURAL ENGINEER Ove Arup & Partners
ART 'Edge of the Trees', First Government House Plaza – Janet Laurence in collaboration with Fiona Foley
SIZE GPT 55,000 square metres, GMT 30,500 square metres, MOS 3,500 square metres
COST GPT AUD\$300 million, GMT AUD\$160 million, MOS AUD\$15 million
ACCESS GPT, GMT (gallery and foyers), MOS – every day, 10.00–18.00

Denton Corker Marshall 1994

City

City

Chifley Tower

The 43-level Chifley Tower addresses Chifley Square on one of Sydney's most elevated sites. Chifley Square was originally conceived as a crescent to mark the changeover from the regular gridded street pattern to its south to the narrower, more winding, diagonally oriented pattern to the north. The latter pattern was the result of both plans by colonial governors and the dictates of the wanderings of the Tank Stream (which now runs underground). The elegant 1950s curtain-walled building, which was formerly Qantas House, was built to curve around the north-western side of the square, but the crescent was never completed.

Although the architectural expression of this building is said by the architects to be 'the result of a concentrated effort involving extensive studies of neighbouring buildings', and a lot of effort has obviously gone into addressing its various façades and levels to different aspects and elements of the cityscape, the final result is a piece of North American classical retro.

Indeed, there are three buildings in Chicago by the architects Kohn Pederson Fox which appear to have influenced the form and expression of Chifley Tower – the near-perfect, tautly curved, green-glass curtain-walled 333 West Wacker Drive of 1983, the neighbouring, vertically-emphasised, rectilinear masonry box of 1989 at number 225, and the 1990 multifaceted, granite and glass tower at 311 South Wacker Drive. In fact, Chifley Tower reads as a conglomeration of features from all of these buildings.

While some aspects of this development – notably the internal gallery of shops, restaurants and cafés – contribute greatly to the life of the city, and its height and profile guarantee it recognition on the city's skyline, the building adds little to Sydney's architectural lexicon and is often criticised.

City

Kohn Pederson Fox/Travis Partners 1992

City

Kohn Pederson Fox/Travis Partners 1992

However, this building should be seen from all sides to appreciate the effort that has gone into making it fully 'contextual'. An excellent distant view of the Chifley Tower, and a full north–south panorama of the city skyline, can be gained from the northern end of Victoria Street in Potts Pont.

ADDRESS Chifley Square
CLIENT Mid Sydney Pty Ltd
STRUCTURAL ENGINEER Flack & Kurtz Australia Pty Ltd
SIZE 72,268 square metres COST AUD$425 million
ACCESS public areas open; wintergarden open 24 hours

Kohn Pederson Fox/Travis Partners 1992

City

Kohn Pederson Fox/Travis Partners 1992

Number One O'Connell Street

This is an above average example of the new breed of contextual, commercial office buildings which in recent years have taken over from the glass and aluminium slab-on-plaza variety. They generally feature a podium, lots of glossy granite on the outside, lavish timber and marble interior spaces and generous amounts of public space, usually in the form of large glassy atriums or arcades with boutiques and/or gourmet multi-cultural food courts. The provision of these amenities is rewarded with generous floor-space bonuses but, even though they are not entirely public, the fad for large internal/external spaces to accommodate Sydney's booming café/restaurant society is adding new dimensions to the city's hierarchy of spaces and creating extraordinary changes in the commercial office block design programme. Developments vary from the downright basic, which can be seen all over town, to the sophisticated chic of this development, which probably represents the state of the commercial art (in respect of design, structure and services) at the height of the 1980s boom. The client wanted a landmark building with an 'establishment' presence, and, although architecturally this building does not push the boundaries (despite some influences from James Stirling's Number 1 Poultry at podium level), it has certainly helped to explode the plan and blur the differences between public and private space.

Three levels of shopping and cafés have access from the different levels of O'Connell and Bent Streets. They snake around the office foyer and culminate in a large exotic 20-metre-high palm-filled 'wintergarden' at the corner of the site – an animated space which, while recalling some of the spatial extravagances of a 1930s movie set, is perfectly suited to the behaviour of young, urban, financial-world professionals.

Externally the podium relates the development to its context – the sandstone-faced Chatsworth House and the Sulman Award-winning

Peddle Thorp Architects 1993

City

Peddle Thorp Architects 1993

Macknade House of 1943 (the façades of which are retained on the site) and the two historic public buildings opposite (the Lands Department and the Education Department buildings).

The tower, small as it is by Sydney standards, cleverly takes advantage of the lie of the land it sits on and an unobstructed view corridor. With its glass-clad cylindrical form and conical domed top emerging from behind thin planes of masonry, it becomes a significant element in the cityscape, particularly from Sydney Cove (Circular Quay).

In the words of the late Michael Dickinson, one of Sydney's most dedicated and prolific architectural writers, 'Serious money became an intensely glamorous matter in the 80s. And in Sydney there are few places where the money is more serious than in O'Connell Street. It needed new glamour. This building provides some. Maybe it's not great architecture but urbane it certainly is.'

ADDRESS 1 O'Connell Street
CLIENT Northbourne Developments Pty Ltd
STRUCTURAL ENGINEER Ove Arup & Partners
SIZE 56,000 square metres COST AUD$150 million
ACCESS to public areas, arcade, wintergarden, lobbies

City

Peddle Thorp Architects 1993

City

Peddle Thorp Architects 1993

Capita Centre

The client's desire to be located in the heart of Sydney's business centre led to an ingenious and exciting design for this small site – 30 metres wide by 42 metres deep and surrounded on three sides by buildings of between 20 and 25 storeys. It was clear that a development on this site would have to generate its own internal source of daylight and outlook. The architect's solution was to divide the floor area into six squares, each approximately 12 by 13 metres. At each level only four of the squares were built on, allowing a third of the building to be hollowed out to its full height by an open atrium which, changing location as it rises through the building, enables all offices to be a maximum of 12 metres from a window overlooking it.

In the lower section of the building the atrium is located against the southern boundary and forms the dramatically high entrance space. In the middle section, the atrium is in the centre, opening to the north, from where it steps progressively outwards towards the boundary, letting sun and daylight penetrate to ground level. At the top, above the height of the adjoining multi-storey buildings, the width of the atrium is along the northern boundary, giving views to the north and east. The stepped profile of the atrium allows sun and natural daylight to reach all the terraces, which are planted lushly throughout with tall palms and fig trees reaching heights of 15 metres. Recessed façade gardens, one or two floors high, also provide relief from the sealed air-conditioned environment and break up the otherwise regular pattern of the façade.

Entering the ground-floor lobby, which has no doors to create a barrier between building and street, is like stepping off the rather bleak urban pavement of Castlereagh Street into a rain forest. The forms at this level are seductively curved and Lin Utzon's platinum and blue porcelain mural forms a brilliant visual backdrop to the whole scene.

Harry Seidler & Associates 1989

City

Harry Seidler & Associates 1989

On the ground floor in the narrow section at the back of the site are a restaurant and mezzanine bar, with the end wall a shimmering 10-metre-high curtain of water.

An exposed steel vertical truss brace-frame energetically zigzags up the 31 floors of the building, punctuating the huge vertical openings and greatly enlivening the street. The truss extends above the roof and supports a 30-metre-high retractable flagpole

This is one of Sydney's best buildings.

ADDRESS 9 Castlereagh Street
CLIENT Capita Insurance
STRUCTURAL ENGINEER Miller Milston & Ferris
SIZE 260,000 square metres COST AUD$110 million
ACCESS to landscaped ground floor (mural by Lin Utzon) and restaurant

Harry Seidler & Associates 1989

City

Harry Seidler & Associates 1989

Ernst & Young Tower

While not a brilliant piece of architecture, this 24-level development demonstrates some of the urban design guidelines introduced by the Sydney City Council in the Western Precinct of the CBD in the late 1980s, when large site amalgamations were beginning to take place and developments were creating huge unresolved gaps in the streetscape. In contrast to the usual and banal developer formula of siting a large high-rise tower seemingly randomly (but usually in a position dictated by best views) and leaving amorphous residue space all around, the guidelines focused on encouraging developments which created useful urban spaces while maintaining the definition of the street.

This development's 17-metre-high stainless steel and glass atrium runs the full length of the Kent Street façade, linking it to Sussex Street and giving a new dimension to the meaning of urban space and movement in the area. The atrium opens up access and outlooks to the west (rare in this north–south oriented city) and encloses a light, airy space which, relaxed and refreshingly free of elaborations and contrivances, serves as plaza, office entry, café area and through route. The delicate, space-frame roof structure is supported at the street front by an open-gridded, granite-clad steel frame which maintains the integrity of the street wall.

Unfortunately, above the atrium, the 19-level sheer glass office building appears blocky, unresolved and unsympathetic. The Sussex Street façade, a sweeping glass curve overlooking Darling Harbour, is more successful.

ADDRESS 321 Kent Street
CLIENT State Authorities Superannuation Board
STRUCTURAL ENGINEER MPN Group Consulting Engineers
SIZE 28,900 square metres COST $100 million
ACCESS to public areas

City

Devine Erby Mazlin 1992

City

Devine Erby Mazlin 1992

The Cornerstone

The Western Precinct of the city, which runs west from York Street, was originally an area of warehouses and associated offices serving the shipping activities of Darling Harbour. In the early 1980s, with a few exceptions, it was still characterised by the elaborate brick façades, generally four to six storeys in height, of late Victorian and early twentieth-century buildings sitting cheek by jowl along the street boundaries. One of the strategies adopted by the City Council to preserve this ambient streetscape in the face of developers' sudden interest in sites overlooking the Darling Harbour development area (fast turning into a reality by 1985) was to create controls and guidelines for the retention of façades which contributed to it. As well as preserving the Victorian flavour, this strategy had the benefit of maintaining a strong building-line along the street boundary, which, as the Council knew from past experience, was always sacrificed when large amalgamated sites were redeveloped.

While this building does not emerge from the podium of retained façades in quite the way Council planners envisaged (buildings which set back as they rose were deemed more appropriate), the contrasting scales and the juxtaposition of old and new are treated in a bold and playful manner, and the elements and devices of the historic façades are used as the basis for the new design without resort to post-modernist pastiche. A terraced ground-floor atrium/food court and access through the site also contribute to the amenity of the precinct.

ADDRESS corner of King and Kent Streets
CLIENT CRI Limited
STRUCTURAL ENGINEER Irwin Johnston Smith Leuchers
SIZE 19,000 square metres COST AUD$40 million
ACCESS open

Philip Cox Richardson Taylor & Partners 1990

Philip Cox Richardson Taylor & Partners 1990

City Bus Shelters/Street Furniture

These elegant, tubular steel-framed bus shelters, with sand-cast aluminium cross-arm roof supports, were designed originally for the Macquarie Street Boulevard project (page 52) as part of a new range of street furniture for both Macquarie Street and the Circular Quay Promenade (page 28). When the City Council, with architects Stephenson and Turner, transformed one of Sydney's major historic monuments – the elaborate, romanesque-style Queen Victoria Building – from musty offices for the Electricity Authority to a major retail centre and transport exchange, the bus shelters were used to complement the building's richly decorative Victorian architecture. They stretch along the York Street façade providing shelter for a major bus terminal interchange.

Before the design of the new range of street furniture, which included seats, benches, bins, lights and eventually a telephone booth, Sydney's streetscape elements had been of the stock-standard, abysmal, local government variety, displaying no consideration for comfort, convenience or beauty. Conybeare Morrison & Partners were conscious of the heritage associations of Circular Quay and Macquarie Streets (in fact both projects were heavily heritage-oriented by their programmes) and their concept was to create a contemporary version of the timeless designs of European street and park furniture.

In an environment of burgeoning civic design-awareness and in the vacuum of street furniture design that existed, the various elements of the well-designed and executed range of elements produced for the two areas had an instant appeal and were used for many other projects by both councils and private developers. The popularity of the street furniture was such that there are now many imitators, generally producing items of lesser design quality and craftsmanship. These have also appeared all over the city and in the suburbs, often in inappropriate situations. Even the

Conybeare Morrison & Partners 1988

Conybeare Morrison & Partners 1988

design for the telephone booth, commissioned by Telecom, has been copied and produced in a clumsy, distorted version of the faintly Victorian original which can be seen all around town.

What was initially perceived as timeless design has thus become somewhat ubiquitous and rather clichéd. Nevertheless, it has radically altered ideas about designing for the public realm, and the architects are currently designing very sleek street furniture with a very contemporary look.

ADDRESS Queen Victoria Building, York and George Streets
CLIENT Department of Public Works (original client)
STRUCTURAL ENGINEER Paterson Wholohan Grill
COST bus shelters – AUD$30,000 each

Conybeare Morrison & Partners 1988

Conybeare Morrison & Partners 1988

Capitol Theatre

Sydney's fetish for façade retention is not such a recent trend. Sections of the Capitol's façade date from the New Belmore Markets of 1893, the city's first formal fruit and vegetable markets, which were dismantled and reconstructed as a hippodrome in 1916. In 1928 the building was restructured internally to the design of John Eberson, a Los Angeles movie-theatre designer. The result was a lavish atmospheric theatre creating the illusion of a palatial Italian garden under a glowing, starry midnight sky. It was probably saved from demolition by the staging of the long-running *Jesus Christ Superstar* which opened in the early 1970s. The lights of the Capitol eventually went out in 1983 when its dilapidated condition and lack of modern facilities made it no longer suitable for theatre use. However, the Royal Australian Institute of Architects' 1986 Capitol Theatre Ideas Competition, which was held in response to the uncertain future of the building, was instrumental in the reassessment of the theatre by its owners, the Sydney City Council, and the subsequent placing of a Permanent Conservation Order on it by the NSW Government. In this latest stage of its evolution the Capitol has been restored, reconstructed and extended to become a first-class, 2,000-seat lyric theatre.

The interiors were restored to the full glory of the 1928 fantasy, and a new stage tower, dressing rooms, green room, rehearsal rooms, foyer and bars were added by extending into Hay Street in a manner which is sympathetic but sufficiently modern to distinguish the addition from the original. The new foyer, a dynamic, brightly-coloured 1990s pastiche of post-modernism with a dash or two of deconstructivism, fails to gel with the brilliance of the illusionistic interior of the theatre. It looks somewhat incongruous with its floor covered with an exact copy of the pastel-coloured, patchy-patterned 1927 carpet.

However, this is a negligible criticism in the face of the fact that this

Peddle Thorp Architects 1995

development has struck a powerful blow for returning life to the southern end of the city centre. New apartment buildings in the precinct have proliferated over the period of the Capitol's flowering, and the massive World Centre Project, which was a gigantic hole in the ground for many years, has also been revived.

ADDRESS Campbell and Hay Streets
CLIENT Ipoh Garden Developments/Sydney City Council
STRUCTURAL ENGINEER Meinhardt (NSW)
COST AUD$24 million
ACCESS foyer Monday to Saturday 9.00–20.00

City

Peddle Thorp Architects 1995

Peddle Thorp Architects 1995

Hotel Nikko

The Hotel Nikko site presented challenging problems, and the form of the building was largely determined by its location and constraints. Long and narrow, with a 210-metre frontage to Sussex Street, the site straddles the southbound lanes of the western distributor freeway and is bounded to the west by its elevated northbound lanes and Darling Harbour. Four two- and three-storey historic buildings on Sussex Street had to be integrated into the project. The architects saw the proposed development as an opportunity to reinforce the edge of the CBD and provide a backdrop to the Darling Harbour Precinct.

The 645-room hotel accommodates its public spaces in a podium structure which, on the Sussex Street side, is formed by the heritage buildings. These are integrated, functionally, into the development by their use as public areas and, physically, by the creation of a narrow, three-storey glazed galleria, which runs behind the central warehouse building, providing dramatic contrasts between its warm brick and sandstone walls and the sleek, smooth surfaces of the new addition.

The hotel accommodation is in two gleaming white slab blocks which stretch along the podium with opposing curvatures, giving the development a light and somewhat nautical image expressive of its location on the water's edge. The convex (viewed from Darling Harbour) slab is 14 levels high above Sussex Street, while the concave section subtly steps down to the north, acknowledging the direction of the CBD peninsula.

ADDRESS 121–185 Sussex Street
CLIENT Shimizu Corporation
STRUCTURAL ENGINEER Lend Lease Design Group
SIZE 35,593 square metres COST AUD$168 million
ACCESS open

City

Lend Lease Design Group/Rice Daubney Group 1992

Lend Lease Design Group/Rice Daubney Group 1992

Darling Harbour

Darling Harbour

The redevelopment of Darling Harbour was the centrepiece of the NSW Government's programme for the 1988 Bicentenary. Immediately to the west of the CBD, the 54-hectare site, originally the centre for the transportation of wool and farm produce, was by the late 1970s a decrepit backwater, inaccessible to the public, largely derelict, and criss-crossed by a tangle of elevated roads. There were many calls to the government for the area to be redeveloped, but they fell on deaf ears.

Early in the 1980s, the energetic American landscape architect, Lawrence Halprin, conducted a weekend workshop in an old woolstore on the site. He persuaded a large group of eminent architects to walk through it blindfolded to 'get its feel' and, later, to dance or act out their impressions and ideas for its use. Perhaps this theatrical approach was prophetic: the following year the Labour-run City Council's hopes for housing and parkland on the site were dashed when the State Premier announced that Darling Harbour would be developed as a 'people's place' – a huge, 24-hour, open-air, pedestrianised entertainment area for the residents of Sydney and its increasing numbers of tourists.

A Development Strategy, produced by the Public Works Department, was exhibited in December 1984. In 1985, the Darling Harbour Authority (which could bypass City Council controls) was established, a Quality Review Committee set up, the MSJ Group appointed as the 'project design directorate', and, unusually for a government-funded scheme, a private firm of contractors appointed to provide services in project management, financial and construction programming, administration and supervision – all part of the fast-track process needed to have Darling Harbour ready for opening in January 1988.

It was a daunting programme. To begin with, the site was an incredible hotchpotch of seemingly impossible obstructions to a fluid design, and,

The MSJ Group 1988

The MSJ Group 1988

to make matters worse, the location and footprint of the main buildings had been laid down in the Development Strategy Plan. MSJ's task was to bring all these elements into meaningful physical and spatial relationships purely through the design of the public domain. This has been achieved by the use of a bold, simple geometry. The Park Green is a large circular form which, by generating two long, narrow axial pathways, sets up a fulcrum at the site's centre and creates dynamic relationships between the centre and all the other major building elements (even the unfortunate Festival Market), despite their general unrelatedness to each other. This strong organising structure defined and linked the public spaces, allowing their design to be filled out according to their specific locational needs.

Cockle Bay was conceived as a water plaza surrounded by a promenade, with the Maritime Museum and Aquarium marking either end and the bridge forming a viewing platform. The expressway was considered a sculptural element and the spaces below it were landscaped with tall cabbage-tree palms, creating a cathedral-like quality. Tumbalong Park was designed for intense usage, with a range of overlapping experiences. The Urban Stream – a modern interpretation of the original stream which ran into Cockle Bay – simulates various stages of a real stream's journey.

MSJ also designed the Palm Pavilion, Central Services Building, Outdoor Stage, the landscaping, lighting, signage, paving and street furniture.

ADDRESS Darling Harbour
CLIENT Darling Harbour Authority
STRUCTURAL ENGINEERS Bond James Laron Murtagh;
Ove Arup & Partners
SIZE 54 hectares COST AUD$20 million
ACCESS open

The MSJ Group 1988

The MSJ Group 1988

Sydney Convention Centre

At first glance, from the east looking across the water, this building is hard to read. The menacing presence of the sprawling Festival Market Place with its undisciplined contours and in-your-face colouring makes it difficult to appreciate immediately the visual pleasures of the Convention Centre's taut, precise form, its subtle compositional modelling and its bold pivotal relationship to the elevated expressway. But when the mind and eye adjust it can be seen that this building is one fine ingredient in the visual mulligatawny which, in this section of Darling Harbour, has resulted from too many chefs too hastily preparing an unfinished recipe.

The brief required that a conference for 3,500 people could be held at the same time as several smaller meetings and functions. The architect's modernist approach is clear and direct, yet it beautifully resolves difficult urban design issues as well as the functional ones of the programme.

Two semi-circular forms face each other at either side of a high, light-filled linear foyer. The smaller of the two (containing restaurant and bar on ground level, foyers and meeting rooms above) addresses the waterfront promenade. With its slender concrete columns rising to support the solid overhanging floor above, it confronts the strong horizontal directionality of the expressway, taming it into an acceptable urban element. The larger semi-circle (banqueting hall below and plenary hall above) is surrounded by eight round towers containing spiralling, double-helix escape stairs, air-conditioning ducts, rainwater pipes and other services.

ADDRESS Darling Drive or Waterfront Promenade
CLIENT Darling Harbour Authority
STRUCTURAL ENGINEER Miller Milston & Ferris
SIZE 27,000 square metres COST AUD$120 million
ACCESS to public areas – dependent on current use

John Andrews International 1988

Darling Harbour

Darling Harbour

John Andrews International 1988

National Maritime Museum

The Maritime Museum and the Sydney Aquarium, facing each other across the water, act as gateways to Darling Harbour, marking the transition from the working port to the playground environment of the redeveloped waterside precinct. Philip Cox has always believed that architecture should express the identity and culture of the city or region in which it is built, and his approach is generally expressive and poetic, using imagery drawn from the local landscape, memories of the area and aspirations for its future. This site, facing towards the city's working port area, provided links between past and present maritime activities.

Cox considered that the architecture of both the Maritime Museum and the Sydney Aquarium (see page 120) required 'a lyrical, even theatrical, expression based on nautical themes', and used the lightness and flexibility of a large-span steel structure to design the museum to look like 'a boat in full sail about to float down the harbour'. Cox has successfully created a lyrical effect in this building, with its large, white billowing roofs stretched out one over the other, almost floating above the concrete podium on which they sit. The museum responds beautifully to its marine environment, and its ascending roofs are also suggestive of the unlimited potential of Sydney's Pyrmont area. These curving, white aluminium-clad forms (the highest is 25 metres) layer towards the waterfront, effectively reducing the building's scale and creating an intimate relationship at pedestrian level.

Internally, the billowing roofs form a series of vaulted spaces that can accommodate exhibits varying from the America's Cup yachts to model ships. (The very sleek minimalist US Gallery by architects Burley Katon Halliday is well worth seeing.)

To provide links between past and present maritime activities, views

Darling Harbour

Philip Cox Richardson Taylor & Partners 1990

Philip Cox Richardson Taylor & Partners 1990

are opened up towards the port through a system of mezzanine levels and glazed panels. Outside, three new piers provide moorings for historic craft.

This is a building that should definitely be viewed from all sides, from the water as well as the land. The northern end is especially joyful. Take a ferry from Circular Quay to Darling Harbour.

Darling Harbour

ADDRESS Darling Harbour
CLIENT Darling Harbour Authority
STRUCTURAL ENGINEER Ove Arup & Partners
SIZE 8,500 square metres COST AUD$36 million
ACCESS open every day

Philip Cox Richardson Taylor & Partners 1990

Darling Harbour

Philip Cox Richardson Taylor & Partners 1990

Sydney Exhibition Centre

One of the major buildings of the Darling Harbour redevelopment, and certainly the biggest, the Exhibition Centre was also the first major building of the genre to be built in Australia. It stretches from freeway to freeway in staggered formation along the western edge of Darling Harbour. Using a steel mast and cable structure, which allowed the long, low horizontal scale, it contains five 5,000-square-metre column-free halls, each 13.5 metres high with clear spans of 60–84 metres. The mast and cable structure is anchored within service zones between each hall and supported by trussed outriggers cantilevered off each main mast. The division of the vast footprint into five distinct areas allowed the building to be operatively viable as well as mediating its great mass.

With this building Philip Cox manifests his interest in creating buildings which are located in time as well as place. He employs state-of-the-art structure to create a building which is innovative technologically and, in the manner of the great nineteenth-century glasshouses, is both expressive and romantic.

A line of large nineteenth-century brick woolstores extends along the cliff face behind the Exhibition Centre forming the canvas against which the gesticulating rhythm of the 20 tall white masts and their accompanying crisp white cables can be read. The Exhibition Centre itself forms a powerful, articulated backdrop to this inner section of the Darling Harbour development, giving significant structural coherence to its urban design while at the same time interacting animatedly with the various other buildings and elements.

The building is raised on a podium to overlook Tumbalong Park, relating to it through the series of stairs rising to the terraced pedestrian thoroughfare which runs the length of the building at mezzanine level. There are views both in and out through the glass-enclosed foyers

Darling Harbour

Philip Cox Richardson Taylor & Partners 1988

which also run the building's full length, and parking for 1,000 cars under the podium.

The total project from design concept to completion took only 32 months, a not altogether surprising fact considering that the interiors are huge empty spaces waiting to be filled.

Despite the vibrancy and animation of this building, and the attempts to integrate it with the rest of Darling Harbour, the Exhibition Centre is often underused and can sometimes look rather bleak and uninhabited.

Darling Harbour

ADDRESS Darling Harbour Drive or Waterfront Promenade
CLIENT Darling Harbour Authority
STRUCTURAL ENGINEER Ove Arup & Partners
SIZE 25,000 square metres plus 1,000 car spaces
COST AUD$80 million
ACCESS to public areas – dependent on current use

Philip Cox Richardson Taylor & Partners 1988

Darling Harbour

Philip Cox Richardson Taylor & Partners 1988

Sydney Aquarium

The Aquarium is one of the trilogy of Darling Harbour buildings designed by the architects as Bicentenary projects.

Forming one side of the harbour gateway to the Darling Harbour development, it uses a vocabulary of curved forms similar to that of the Maritime Museum to announce the departure from the utilitarian port which abuts it to the north. The building sits on an old timber pier that extends into the harbour and runs perpendicular to the museum.

The Aquarium complex has three main components. Above ground on Pier 26 is the main building with entry, public facilities and display for specific marine habitats. To its north the three floating, semi-submerged tanks of the Oceanarium provide an underwater viewing circuit. On the northern wharf are the support facilities comprising workshops, laboratories, offices and filtration system. While this building is the most spectacular of the three sections, the floating tanks are the focus of the exhibition. Here visitors obtain a real underwater experience of marine life. They can come face to face with the Great White Shark, enormous stingrays, and fantasy fish from the Great Barrier Reef as well as the local Sydney Harbour variety. At close range they can observe 5,000 fish from 600 species going through their daily routine.

Although a friendly place, the maritime imagery of the main building, with its voluptuous, wavy, white roof attenuated along the pier and its sharply sheared-off ends, is so pronounced, particularly if viewed from above, that to some observers it has the uneasy sensuousness of a sleek, high-tech missile poised on the deck of an aircraft carrier. However, viewed from the Pyrmont side of Darling Harbour, the Aquarium is an elegant reminder of the old working finger wharves which graced the edges of the western side of the city when the east–west streets ran straight down to the waterfront.

Philip Cox Richardson Taylor & Partners 1988

Philip Cox Richardson Taylor & Partners 1988

The main building contains interpretive displays in a sequential storyline through floors which overlap and open up to harbour views to enhance the aquatic experience. The structure of the building is relatively simple. Lightweight prefabricated steel frames at 7.2-metre centres are cantilevered off the existing pier slab and conventional metal sheeting supported by steel purlins forms the curved roof.

Darling Harbour

ADDRESS Pier 26, Darling Harbour
CLIENT Jonray Holdings
STRUCTURAL ENGINEER Ove Arup & Partners
SIZE 2,355 square metres; two oceanariums, each 760 square metres
COST AUD$22 million
ACCESS open every day, 9.30–21.00

Philip Cox Richardson Taylor & Partners 1988

Darling Harbour

Philip Cox Richardson Taylor & Partners 1988

Hotel Ibis and Darling One Apartments

This development sits on top of an existing car park on a site which forms part of the north-western boundary of Darling Harbour. The 16-level residential building (with 215 apartments) and the 11-storey two-star hotel (with 256 rooms) were built as one project, and are linked visually by the car park, the continuous first three floors, and a large wall which rolls down from the roof of the apartments to the roof of the hotel like a section through a giant wave.

Although the development has been heavily criticised for creating a visual and physical barrier between the city and the Ultimo/Pyrmont area (currently being regenerated), it actually conforms to the urban design guidelines imposed by the Darling Harbour Authority, which, naturally enough, wanted a backdrop to the Darling Harbour development. Unlike its neighbour (the unfortunate Novotel, which appears to have been shaped to the exact outline of a simplistic building envelope), this development, while obviously commercial in intent and execution, has strongly articulated façades. The considered complexity and intricate interplay of windows, balconies, recesses, curves, colours and materials give the building a visual interest which ameliorates the impact of its bulk.

Along the eastern face of the ground floor is a wide paved terrace which also acts as a viewing platform overlooking Darling Harbour and a public walkway linking Murray Street, Darling Harbour and the Novotel.

ADDRESS Murray Street, Pyrmont
CLIENT Citistate Corporation
STRUCTURAL ENGINEER Acer Wargon Chapman
SIZE hotel – 8,616 square metres; apartments – 29,489 square metres
COST AUD$70 million
ACCESS to public areas

Darling Harbour

Travis Partners/Hoffer Reid & Coombs 1994

Travis Partners/Hoffer Reid & Coombs 1994

Eastern Suburbs

Tusculum

Architect John Verge's 1830s neoclassical villa is the home of the NSW Chapter of the Royal Australian Institute of Architects and was acquired for a peppercorn rent from the Historic Houses Trust in 1984. The sale of its previous building enabled the Institute to restore Tusculum for use as meeting rooms, conference and exhibition facilities and a bookshop, and to erect a new building on the site for offices and a lecture theatre.

Levine and Durbach's scheme is the result of a design competition which stressed the twin principles of respect for the historic villa and confidence in contemporary architecture. Their design, a visual treatise illustrating an infinite number of ideas on how modern and historic buildings can co-exist, provides lessons which have often gone unheeded since. Rather than use materials, proportions and rhythms similar to the historic building – as the current common wisdom of conservation demands –the architects seized on the opportunity to create vivid contrasts.

The main wall of the new building runs in a convex curve at the rear of the site, providing a solid asymmetrically pierced backdrop to the regular rhythms and recesses of Tusculum's façade. The entry, off the point where the two buildings meet at a right angle, is high and glassy and, although barely visible until the imposing formal entry of the old building has been passed, is the fulcrum of a number of powerful, overlapping visual and spatial experiences. Upstairs, a terraced outdoor room, sitting like a small amphitheatre, faces Tusculum's rear wall.

ADDRESS 3 Manning Street, Potts Point
CLIENT NSW Chapter, Royal Australian Institute of Architects
STRUCTURAL ENGINEER Miller Milston & Ferris
SIZE 300 square metres COST AUD$1.3 million
ACCESS open Monday to Friday 9.00–17.00

Eastern Suburbs

Levine & Durbach/Allen Jack + Cottier 1986

Levine & Durbach/Allen Jack + Cottier 1986

Box Café and Darley Street Thai

The Box Café is slotted into a long, narrow space between two restaurants. In contrast to the inconspicuous storeroom which had occupied the site, the Box Café, with full-gloss ice-green walls and ceiling, stainless steel floor and small kreon lights bouncing dazzling reflections off the shiny surfaces, is a beautifully controlled, minimalist space and a glowing presence on the street. With leather-upholstered banquette seating fitting into recesses in the walls, the Box is just wide enough for eight small tables and 12 zebrano timber veneer box-shape stools. A mirrored wall at the end of the space extends it visually, giving reflective glimpses of the tiny stainless steel galley kitchen and adding a sense of mystery.

In the next-door Darley Street Thai, the hot and cold bold colours of the walls and the progression through a sequence of spaces, which is measured dramatically by rows of black rendered columns and circular cutout skylights, evoke not only the opulence but the serenity and order of Thai temples and religious processions. Originally a series of Victorian rooms, the spaces were extended and unified with a rear courtyard which is as formalised and controlled as the other three spaces in the restaurant. In the courtyard a lime-green wall clashes perfectly with the hot-pink wall and banquette of one of the interior spaces. The experience of colour and texture which interweaves the formality and order is introduced at the door by the gold-leaf-covered vestibule.

ADDRESS 30 Bayswater Road, Kings Cross
CLIENT Box Café – Iain Halliday and David Katon; Darley Street Thai – David Thompson and Peter Bower
SIZE Box Café – 24 square metres; Darley Street Thai – 140 square metres
COST Box Café – AUD$60,000; Darley Street Thai – AUD$400,000
ACCESS open

Burley Katon Halliday 1995 and 1994

House Podle

The original house on this site was burned down in a Guy Fawkes Night conflagration when the owners were away. The site itself was difficult – small and triangular, on the side of a cliff, tightly bounded by higher buildings to the north and south, and accessible only via a long, narrow path from the road below. Three streams ran across the site, and an historic 5-metre-high, convict-built sandstone retaining wall divided it diagonally into two angled sections on different levels. Rather than being viewed as constraints, however, these features of the site provided the catalyst for the design concept.

The essence of the design lies in the use of a series of overlaying and interlocking planes. From the front of the site there is a stepped progression of spaces which, connected by staircases, bridges, balconies and terraces, lead the visitor from the street to the house, and eventually to a lap pool on the upper site level – in the words of the architect, 'a necklace of spaces which you can traverse seamlessly, forwards or backwards, up or down, indoors or outdoors'.

Designed as two distinct but connected two-storey pavilions, which splay apart to accommodate a triangular entry court and circulation zone between them, the house contains no corridors. Living areas are in a large double-height space in the northern pavilion, divided into zones by changes in floor levels rather than walls; matching upstairs and downstairs bedrooms are contained in the southern pavilion.

ADDRESS 21a New Beach Road, Rushcutters Bay
STRUCTURAL ENGINEER Taylor Thomson Whitting
SIZE 160 square metres COST AUD$350,000
ACCESS none

Neil Durbach Architect 1993

Neil Durbach Architect 1993

Watsons Bay House

An ingeniously simple geometric plan transforms a rather ordinary (except for its harbour view and splendid large eucalypt) rectangular suburban site into the base from which a voluptuous, glowing beacon of a house emerges. In its commanding location close to the street, the curving geometry of this three-storey house allows it to take full advantage of space, sun, light and views, and to resonate internally with the energy of its perfectly controlled flow of space.

The front and rear opposing corners of a basically square plan are cut off by quadrants eliminating two right-angled areas of 'dead space'. At the middle level these frameless curved-glass arcs enclose a space which flows continuously to the other two corners (used as a seating area and study) and around the curved walls of the focal element of the interior (the spiral stair). One ascends and descends this elegant staircase in a cylinder of light which pierces the centre of the building.

The spatial movement throughout the house is emphasised by the use of glass doors and walls (solid walls are kept to a minimum) to separate the living, family, dining and study areas. A doubly curved, prestressed-concrete balcony projects from the north-facing wall, superimposing a directional dimension on the internal spaces. On the southern side the glass arc opens directly on to garden and swimming pool. The upper floor contains four bedrooms; the ground level comprises entrance, garage and playroom. Walls are concrete block, specially formulated to expose selected aggregate on their external, polished surfaces.

ADDRESS 25 Palmerston Street, Vaucluse
STRUCTURAL ENGINEER Birzulis Associates
SIZE 250 square metres COST AUD$630,000
ACCESS none

Eastern Suburbs

Harry Seidler & Associates 1994

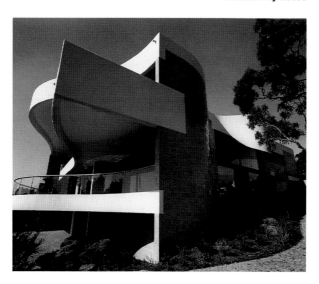

Harry Seidler & Associates 1994

Vaucluse House

On a hilltop in one of Sydney's most prestigious suburbs, the site of this house commands spectacular views of the city skyline and the shoreline on the other side of the harbour. To take advantage of these views, the owners demolished their previous residence on the site to build a luxurious, two-storey house behind the huge old angophora tree which was retained in the centre of the entrance drive court at the top of the site.

The essentially rectangular plan sets up spaces in a symmetrical formalised manner which is uncharacteristic of Harry Seidler's work. The large entry foyer, with a top-lit spiral stair at its centre, leads directly into the dining space, with living room and study opening to the left, and kitchen areas, utilities and games room in a block to the right. So far, so formal – but these luxuriously proportioned spaces are articulated as purely modern, and at various points are energised by the expansion of the straight line into billowing curves which act and interact, play and interplay, and create, externally, an overall form of sheer dynamism in which there is not a trace of the formal or static.

The second level contains three large bedrooms with bathrooms, one with its own sitting room/study and a servant's apartment. Materials are solid and permanent. External walls of polished, precast-concrete blocks support prestressed-concrete floors. The living areas are paved with highly polished Indian Tamin granite slabs, which are also used on fireplace walls and the tops of furniture units.

ADDRESS 48 Wentworth Road, Vaucluse
STRUCTURAL ENGINEER Birzulis Associates
SIZE 615 square metres plus 110 square metres for garages and plant
ACCESS none

Harry Seidler & Associates 1990

Harry Seidler & Associates 1990

Lloyd-Jones House

The design of this house involved the transformation of a 1910 free-standing, two-storey brick corner shop and, to guarantee a private court-yard garden, the purchase of an adjoining property. The building was demolished, except for the side street wall, and replaced by a 'gentleman's residence' with main reception/library and kitchen/dining room contained on the ground floor in a vast gallery, 22 metres long, 6 metres wide and 5 metres high. The master bedroom/dressing room is on a half level above the gallery, and on the top floor there is a private living room with terraces overlooking the harbour to the west and the ocean to the east.

The gallery is the space-defining and form-giving element of the house. Its volume shapes the external form and interacts with all the other spaces, both internal and external. With its reverse-shear prow front and double-height glazed northern wall, the building sits in a large water garden with the aplomb and elegance of a sleek, white vessel. A ribbed, curved roof cantilevers out over the glass wall, reinforcing the marine imagery. In addition, like a giant unfolding lotus flower, it also reinforces the serenity of the setting.

From the smallest details to the largest shapes and forms, there is a strong interplay of elements in this highly articulate building, which is read both internally and externally against the space of the gallery. A discordant note is the cantilevered projection of the bedroom, which lacks the refinement of the rest of the building and fails to participate in the interplay.

ADDRESS 294 Old South Head Road, Watsons Bay
STRUCTURAL ENGINEER Birzulis Associates
SIZE 450 square metres
ACCESS none

Graham Jahn Architect 1990

Graham Jahn Architect 1990

Ristorante Mario

When it required more space, Mario's moved around the corner from its Stanley Street address into this large disused 1930s car showroom which, with steel-trussed saw-tooth roof, was virtually column-free and had superb natural lighting from large runs of windows on three sides.

A new entrance at the corner was designed to focus the mind on the transition from street to restaurant. The sense of entry is heightened by the ascent of a small flight of stairs against rough textured walls and the directional emphasis of the elongated sheet-copper canopy which glides overhead and emerges into the bright openness of the restaurant.

The restaurant space is broken up into four main zones, but its overall visual unity is maintained by a system of horizontal layering which interfaces with strategically located elements, allowing space to flow through and around the shell of the building without letting its verticality predominate. The reception/bar, the most important object in the lower layer, is large, open and horizontally emphasised. Light-green below and topped with slabs of honed white marble, it has a floating white ceiling above and is the visual focus of the restaurant and the element to which everything else relates.

Seating areas are not downplayed. Defined by the low, white, free-standing serpentine wall, the colonnaded screen or the bar itself, they are connected by volumes of space and light. The whole ensemble is bathed with a pale almost iridescent glow which allows the diners themselves to shine brightly.

ADDRESS 38 Yurong Street, East Sydney
CLIENT Delzio Pty Ltd
SIZE 470 square metres
ACCESS open for lunch and dinner

Eastern Suburbs

Gordon & Vallich Architects 1995

Gordon & Vallich Architects 1995

Kerridge Wallace Warehouse

This project comprises the renovation of one of a pair of warehouse buildings, linked by a common courtyard, which were built around 1900 as coach repair workshops. The decaying property was bought by the architect and her engineer partner to convert into a residence and office. The external shell of the building was kept in its original state, 'raw and crust-like', and completed with a new large, volumetric, double-curved mansard roof which gracefully complements the classical curves and rhythms of the façade and adds extra scale to the interior. New external materials, such as lead for the roof and rusted steel for the entry, were chosen for their oxidisation and weathering properties – 'to give a painterly dimension to the external fabric'. The overall effect also gives a whiff of faded European grandeur to a tight, narrow street packed with tiny terraces.

The soft patina of the exterior gives no clues as to what to expect inside. One enters into an interior that is bright and open, etched with the clean lines of sharply defined and brightly coloured geometric shapes and forms which juxtapose with the texture of the brick walls and the womb-like curve of the ceiling. Throughout the building this confident combination of hard and soft surfaces and the calculated contrasts of dark and light spaces bring about a volatile spatial dynamic.

The building is divided into three distinct zones of activity. On the mezzanine level are the bedrooms; on the middle level the entry, living area and kitchen; and below is the office, which connects directly with the garden.

ADDRESS 24 Taylor Street, Darlinghurst
STRUCTURAL ENGINEER Philip Wallace
SIZE 250 square metres
ACCESS none

Eastern Suburbs

Virginia Kerridge Architect 1994

Virginia Kerridge Architect 1994

Krempff House

A twist to the old story of young architects getting started by designing a house for their parents (Sir Richard Rogers, Harry Seidler, for example), is that young architects in Sydney are now getting their start by designing much-acclaimed houses for themselves (see also previous entry). The conversion of a rundown Victorian corner-store building into a house for herself, builder-husband and young child was the catalyst for Margaret Krempff to establish her own architectural practice.

The building's lengthy three-storey façade gives no indication of its internal transformation. Because of problems of subsidence and structural integrity, a new steel-framed body, comprising three levels of living space, a courtyard, parking space and a large roof deck, was constructed behind the external shell. Entry is directly off the street. There is then a progression of spatial experiences as one is drawn obliquely into the body of the building, past the spiralling staircase with its snaking, steel support and view of the leafy courtyard, along the space between the double-height curved glass wall and the kitchen and into the multi-angled, multi-sided living space. These spaces, and the elements within them, are given focus and cohesion by the impeccably crafted, brushbox-framed, glazed wall which bows into the courtyard at the pivotal point of the approximately L-shaped plan and links the studio and bridge of the first floor into the spatial composition.

Throughout, straight lines, slanted angles and curves join with deliberate juxtapositions of materials to generate a rich interior.

ADDRESS 465 Liverpool Street, Darlinghurst
STRUCTURAL ENGINEER Partridge Partners Pty Ltd
SIZE 240 square metres COST AUD$420,000
ACCESS telephone for appointment to view: (02) 360 2251

Margaret Krempff Architect 1995

Margaret Krempff Architect 1995

Henwood House

In the desirable inner-city suburb of Paddington the residents live in narrow, restored, two-storey, late-Victorian, speculator-built terrace houses. Although their cast-iron lace balconies make them visually appealing, these buildings generally suffer from a severe lack of internal light. While alterations can ameliorate the situation, the desire to preserve Paddington's charm led the Council to adopt strict regulations protecting original buildings from visible change and requiring infill buildings to be almost exact imitations. Architect Alexander Tzannes could not accept that a plan which was unsuitable for today's needs should be adopted for new buildings. Over a period of ten years, as architect for a number of houses in Paddington, he has fought for a more innovative approach to building design, and developed a radically different solution.

The Henwood House was the first Tzannes house in Paddington – and caused bitter clashes with the Council. More solid and sombre than the typical Paddington terrace, and completely undecorated externally, it is a three-storey building which fits elegantly into the two-storey street, holding the parapet line of its neighbours and stacking unbelievable amounts of space on to a 5.5-metre-wide site. Internally there is no resemblance to a Victorian terrace whatsoever – space and light reign. In section there are four vertical zones – a strip of service rooms against the street; the stair rising in a light-flooded void; kitchen and dining areas, with bedrooms and terraces above; and a single-storey living room which looks on to a large paved inner court contained by the garage at the rear.

ADDRESS 159 Windsor Street, Paddington
STRUCTURAL ENGINEER Taylor Thomson Whitting
SIZE 220 square metres
ACCESS none

Alexander Tzannes 1985

Alexander Tzannes 1985

Holmes, Nursey and Duchen Houses

The sequence of Alexander Tzannes' interventions in Paddington can be seen in a short stroll around the area. In the Holmes House, the second to be built, he exploited the levels of the site to fit four storeys of spacious, light-filled accommodation within the average parapet height of the street, and almost doubled the floor-space ratio, convincing the authorities that greater density than the codes allowed did not have to mean less amenity, and no frills externally did not have to mean loss of delight.

The Nursey House (illustrated) was the third in the Paddington series. The site is atypical, almost twice as wide as the neighbouring subdivisions, and the façade steps in plan and section to reduce bulk and mediate between the adjoining buildings. Like his other houses, the exterior is characterised by a simple masonry treatment using concrete and an integral oxide-coloured finish to the walls. The interior is based on the court-yard plan, and much of the furniture is also designed by the architect.

For the Duchen residence, the Council permitted the use of steel on the façade, allowing a third storey to be added. The building is designed around a pool and courtyard which completely separate the garage and self-contained flat at the rear from the main accommodation.

In all the houses, doors and windows fold away, opening the spaces from front to back. Internal skylights add further light to the central areas, and upper-level landscaped terraces provide views and privacy.

ADDRESS Holmes House, 124 Hargrave Street; Nursey House, 115 Sutherland Street; Duchen House, 77 Sutherland Street
STRUCTURAL ENGINEER Sinclair Knight
SIZE Holmes House – 198 square metres; Nursey House – 368 square metres; Duchen House – 326 square metres
ACCESS none

Alexander Tzannes 1988–95

Alexander Tzannes 1988–95

Berkelouw Bookshop

The Berkelouw Bookshop has been selling second-hand books in Sydney since the Second World War. The building procured for its new premises – on a busy corner opposite another popular bookshop, and on the wrong side of the trendy Paddington main street and just beyond the reach of the lively Taylor's Square area – required a spectacular treatment to draw people across the road. The architects' design for a new three-storey shop front has turned this ordinary early 1900s masonry building into one of the more arresting landmarks of the area.

An apparently seamless glass wall rises over the first two floors and curves around the corner, revealing the shop's interiors and the slender double-height steel columns which support the solid, horizontally expressed second floor above. With this simple design concept the new shop front has become a vertical volume of light, space and activity in an otherwise not very interesting streetscape.

A new open staircase at the centre of the shop allows views between floors, and a café, which is perched on the first floor overlooking the Paddington street life, is visible from the street, creating a further enticement to enter.

Eastern Suburbs

ADDRESS 19 Oxford Street, Paddington
CLIENT Berkelouw Bookshop
COST AUD$600,000
ACCESS open

McConnell Rayner 1994

McConnell Rayner 1994

Verona Cinema Centre

This building is located in one of Sydney's major leisure areas, at the junction between the tawdry but vibrant Taylor's Square and the more affluent, gentrified Paddington. The Verona Cinema Centre brief called for a mixed-use development in an existing 1940s two-storey, brick-clad, concrete-structured industrial building. The architects added two floors, creating a building which comprises retail on the ground floor, a café and yoga centre on the first floor, a quad cinema on the second and third floors, and a penthouse office/apartment at the street edge of the third floor.

The vertical shaft of the stair to the cinema penetrates and connects all the areas. Externally the shaft is topped by a two-sided glass lantern which, set in a steel frame with the building's cooling towers, creates an interesting streetscape feature. Circulation to the cinema is circuitous, weaving up and around the original concrete structure, past a series of zinc-clad boxes containing a light prism, the box office, lift and toilets. The consistent element of this path is the glass, three-storey light prism which rises up through the building next to the stair. Filled with fluorescent-batten fittings, it is the light source for the public spaces and the beacon leading to the cinema.

Externally, various metal-clad forms have been added to the original building (the rooftop additions are wrapped in stainless steel and the awning is sheathed in copper) – these are combined 'in a frantic manner to hint at the building's internal intensity of activities'.

ADDRESS 17 Oxford Street, Paddington
CLIENT Robert Bleakley
STRUCTURAL ENGINEER Connell Wagner Rankine Hill
SIZE 2,135 square metres COST AUD$5 million
ACCESS open

Eastern Suburbs

Tonkin Zulaikha 1996

Tonkin Zulaikha 1996

Uniting Church Manse and Elsbury House

The development on this important corner in Woollahra has been treated as an exercise in urban design. Not only does it provide a new streetscape, but it also creates a public open space and pedestrian link through the site. The new house for the Minister of the Uniting Church and his family also contains community and counselling rooms with a separate entrance. It occupies a triangular allotment and is designed with a skewed L-shaped plan around a private courtyard. The second stage of the development – to be completed by mid-1997 – replaces a brick bungalow and comprises five three-storey townhouses overlooking a 900-square-metre landscaped common which will give direct access to Queen Street, the main shopping street in the area.

Adjoining the Manse is the earlier two-storey Elsbury House. Also roughly L-shaped and dog-legged in plan, it extends around a series of ground-level courtyards and a swimming pool, and contains a separate flat with a designer's studio and large landscaped terrace above at the rear.

Externally both houses are quite unlike Tzannes' interventions in Paddington, expressing the different site conditions and the more open physical environment of Woollahra. However, like the Paddington houses, their character and architectural vocabulary are not typical of the area, although entirely compatible and extremely well considered. Rather than being confrontational, they gently and subtly remould the existing built form and could well become a model for new housing in the area.

ADDRESS 111 and 113 Jersey Road, Woollahra
STRUCTURAL ENGINEER Manse – James Taylor & Associates
SIZE Manse – 310 square metres; Elsbury House – 550 square metres
ACCESS Manse – to community areas; Elsbury House – none

Alexander Tzannes 1995, 1992

Alexander Tzannes 1995, 1992

Bistro Moncur and Woollahra Hotel

One of Paddington's favourite eating places was designed as part of the refurbishment of an existing 1937 corner hotel and involved the almost complete rebuilding of the one-storey restaurant which had been built in the original 'pub beer garden'. The design of the hotel section returned the building's fabric to its original condition where possible, but played with internal openings and windows to expand the spatial and visual experience internally and to create qualities of lightness and transparency and a sense of interaction with the street. A new timber bar was designed on the horseshoe principle and located in the centre to refocus the space.

The bistro, set back and elevated slightly above the street, has a narrow outdoor terrace running its full length, roofed with a cable-stayed, taut, white skillion canopy. All the buzz and activity of the busy bistro can be observed from the street through the glazed front wall and are read against the strong, simple forms and surfaces of the interior.

The restaurant space is rectangular, twice as long as it is wide, and its directional quality is emphasised by the expression of strong horizontal lines – the timber bar running along one side, the timber wall panelling which rises to dado level, and the black and white, 1-metre-high graphic by Michael Fitzjames which runs the length of the opposite wall. A long, horizontal opening behind the bar extends the space visually into the pub, and the use of mirrors and a mixture of transparent and translucent glass add to its ambiguities.

ADDRESS Moncur and Queen Streets, Woollahra
CLIENT Ron White and Damien Pignolet
STRUCTURAL ENGINEER James Taylor & Associates
SIZE 582 square metres
ACCESS open Monday to Sunday

Federation Pavilion

By the 1960s the elaborately ornamented Victorian pavilion, built in Centennial Park to celebrate Australia's Federation in 1901, had fallen into total disrepair, leaving only the Commonwealth Stone, a hexagonal granite block standing on a sandstone pedestal, to mark the spot where Australia officially became a nation. In 1984 a limited competition was held for the design of a new monument which would incorporate this symbolic stone. Alexander Tzannes' winning scheme has been both acclaimed and criticised – the criticism mainly for what is perceived as an absence of Australianness and contemporaneity in the architecture and its lack of recognition of Australian landscape. Although on first impression the dedicated modernist may want to decry this building, it is worthwhile taking a closer look to discern the ways in which the architecture elucidates the meaning of the stone and federation. The design is consciously related to the history and symbolism of the site, but rather than celebrate a natural, empty landscape, it sets out to affirm Australia's civilised life and the broad sweep of its history. It is a synthesis of architecture, landscape and art, which are all imbued with reflections on history, culture and the spirit of the place. This monument recognises its function as contemplative: to criticise its architecture as a manifestation of a particular style would imply only a superficial observation of it.

Externally the pavilion is solid and self-contained. With its low graceful dome and stocky sandstone columns, it sits serenely, almost diminutively, in a large grassy clearing encircled by the spreading canopies of Moreton Bay figs. Within the clearing the pavilion is surrounded by a circle of mown grass, like the reflection of its aura. It also conjures up images of Christo and Jeanne-Claude's encircled islands. The six openings in the precast-concrete walls and six sets of paired columns give the pavilion a slightly oscillating effect, as though it has just landed.

Alexander Tzannes 1988

Alexander Tzannes 1988

Internally the floor pattern and ceiling grid reflect the geometry of the protected stone. The sloping, red-granite walls and floor create a dynamic space, the focus of which is the ceiling dome. Raised on fine stainless steel-clad supports, it gives the illusion of hovering above the internal drum. For its underside, 1,440 individual steel plates were painted in vitreous enamel and then put in place, like a mosaic. The design (depicting pain, death and resurrection) was then covered with copper to form the dome's structure. The artwork is thus an integral component of the architecture.

Landscape design is also an essential part of the concept. To emphasise the valley, the land form was altered to make a 100-metre-long funnel-shape, spreading out from an elliptical, arena-like amphitheatre set in the wilder, higher part of the park. Further definition is given by the planting of North American elm trees, which sweep down the hill to the pavilion. This creates a perfect belvedere from which to view the pavilion and the surrounding landscape, and to take in longer, wider views to Botany Bay.

Chiselled on the pavilion's exterior frieze are the words of Australian historian, Professor Manning Clark, paraphrasing Federation poet Bernard O'Dowd – 'Mammon or Millennial Eden'. Palimpsest or conundrum? Whichever, this building is certainly not period pastiche.

ADDRESS Centennial Park
CLIENT Premier's Department of State Government
ARTIST Imants Tillers
LANDSCAPE ARCHITECT Walter Barda
STRUCTURAL ENGINEER Ove Arup & Partners
SIZE total area 200 metres by 70 metres; pavilion 22 metres diameter
COST AUD$1.76 million
ACCESS open

Eastern Suburbs

Alexander Tzannes 1988

Alexander Tzannes 1988

Sydney Football Stadium

There was considerable opposition to the proposal for a new sports ground on this site from nearby residents, who already suffered from noise and traffic generated by the adjacent Sydney Cricket Ground and Showground. Reducing the scale and impact of the stadium was an important consideration in the design process and it has resulted in a spectacular swirl of a building. From the residential areas and approaches to the stadium, the giant, white cantilevered roof seemingly floats above its barely visible, low-slung brick-faced base. Supported on a tubular steel triangulated space-frame truss, the roof sweeps up, swells out and swoops down over seating for 40,000 spectators in a roller coaster of continuous movement which defines the shape of an ellipse cut out of a circle and unifies the internal space with a sense of containment.

The warping of the roof also gave other benefits. It allowed a more efficient structure and avoided excessive shading of the playing area. Field lighting runs along its continuous edge, eliminating the need for huge lighting towers which inevitably spill light over into surrounding areas. The playing field is 3 metres below natural ground level, further reducing height and emphasising the unity and containment of the space. Since the rectangular field runs north–south, the roof is widest to the east and west over the grandstands, where viewing is optimal. The distance between seating and the sidelines ranges from only 8 metres at playing level to 30 metres at the top of the 30-degree-angle grandstands.

ADDRESS Moore Park Road, Paddington
CLIENT Civil & Civic for Sydney Cricket & Sportsground Trust
STRUCTURAL ENGINEER Ove Arup & Partners
COST AUD$62 million
ACCESS open

Philip Cox Richardson Taylor & Partners 1994

Philip Cox Richardson Taylor & Partners 1994

Samuels Building

This was the first new building on the University of New South Wales campus for more than a decade. The brief, expanded after the architects' assessment of the site's potential, called for a building with semi-basement car parking, six levels of accommodation with the ability to be used as research laboratories, and a rooftop glasshouse for the School of Botany.

The upper campus, where the Samuels Building is situated, features a collection of large, almost brutalist, off-form concrete structures of the 1960s and 70s, sited randomly with little thought for the creation of a public realm. The new building was designed to enliven and urbanise this area. Picking up some of the structural rhythms of the surrounding buildings, it stretches low along the street front and curves around the eastern end of the site, providing a conscious urban form which has the effect of uniting the other buildings into a more cohesive relationship. Sitting on the one-storey brick base, the silvery-grey metal-clad walls of the upper six floors are overlaid with a finely detailed screen of cast aluminium elements, creating a pattern that animates the façade with plays of light and shade. The curved end progressively peels back from the base, producing a layering effect which gives the building a streamlined form.

The planning is simple and logical. The structural grid divides the building down the centre into 2- by 7-metre-wide bays: laboratories on one side of the corridor; offices, cool rooms and cores on the other.

ADDRESS University of NSW, Library Road, Gate 11, Botany Street, Randwick
CLIENT University of NSW
STRUCTURAL ENGINEER Ove Arup & Partners
SIZE 70,000 square metres COST AUD$13.7 million including fitouts
ACCESS to public areas

Lawrence Nield & Partners 1991

Lawrence Nield & Partners 1991

Australian Graduate School of Management

Until this extension was completed, the school occupied an undistinguished 1970s building on the University of NSW's upper campus. With this development, wedged in between the existing premises and the carpark façade of the Matthew's building (which looms over it to the west), the architects have given the school a new image and a functional building which ameliorates the adverse aspects of the site. One façade of the L-shaped extension runs along the lane at the rear of the site, the other sits into the hill alongside its overbearing neighbour. The inside of this right-angled block is cut away in a chopped-off elliptical shape by a three-storey-high glazed arcade which curves around an internal courtyard between the old and new buildings in a modern interpretation of the traditional university quadrangle. Inside this a lower metal structure of the same elliptical form hooks back in the opposite direction as a pergola, increasing the sense of linkage between the two buildings. The courtyard becomes the focus of the school's activity, integrating the existing school with the new section and relieving its deadening design.

The new building contains seminar rooms, administration and additional library space. Along the western site boundary it rises five levels – in a rectangular form with polished concrete-block walls – to meet and integrate with the five levels of the existing building.

ADDRESS University of NSW, Gate 11, Botany Street, Randwick (or Oval Lane entry)
CLIENT Australian Graduate School of Management
STRUCTURAL ENGINEER Taylor Thomson Whitting
SIZE 3,000 square metres COST AUD$8 million
ACCESS to courtyard and foyers

Lawrence Nield & Partners 1995

Eastern Suburbs

Lawrence Nield & Partners 1995

University Walk

University Walk is an urban design project, based on the University's masterplan by Jackson Teece Chesterman Willis, which has transformed the upper, eastern section of the campus of the University of NSW. An area characterised by unrelated, unattractive 1960s and 70s buildings and desolate spaces, through which it was extremely difficult and unpleasant to navigate, has become a carefully composed, energetic sequence of places. Connected by a series of covered links, they form a pedestrian spine along the length of the upper campus, providing access from the upper to the lower campus and creating a range of new environments, functions and meanings.

The project comprised the redesign of four large open spaces – Matthews Plaza, Library Lawn, Commerce Courtyard and Basser Steps – and their development as part of an intelligent route through the campus. Extending from Chancellory Road (near the Botany Street entry), University Walk includes a double-level retail arcade, a 400-seat dining pavilion, a single-level covered way in front of Library Lawn, a dual-level covered walkway, a large food court, a viewing and dining rotunda, and a new covered connection to Basser Steps. It also provides wheelchair access to both campuses.

The route ends at the new quadrangle at the foot of the Basser Steps and the whole concept rather fizzles out at this point, beyond which the buildings of the older campus are more formally laid out and the access is more legible. In a later stage of the development, these spaces will also be redesigned and upgraded and the University Walk will extend the length of the campus.

The architectural solution to the varying requirements of the Walk lay in the use of a lightweight steel, vaulted structure which adapts to form pavilions, shelters and covered ways. The latter are punctuated

Conybeare Morrison & Partners 1994

Eastern Suburbs

Conybeare Morrison & Partners 1994

by a series of special structures that highlight particular places and culminate in the glass-enclosed rotunda overlooking the western campus. By unifying and integrating the upper and lower campuses, University Walk has created a new focus for the university and a new way of life for the students.

ADDRESS University of NSW, Gate 11, Botany Street Entry, Randwick
CLIENT University of NSW
LANDSCAPE ARCHITECT Context/Conybeare Morrison & Partners
STRUCTURAL ENGINEERS Paterson Wholohan Grill; Woodcolts, Stace Consulting Engineers
COST AUD$10 million
ACCESS open

Eastern Suburbs

Conybeare Morrison & Partners 1994

Conybeare Morrison & Partners 1994

Centres for Environmental Research

This is the proverbial 'decorated shed'. The users of the building, a group of industry-associated centres at the cutting edge of environmental research technology, required not only additional space at their existing engineering laboratory on the upper campus at the University of NSW, but a new image as well. Also, the basic brick and metal-clad workshop was dominated by the large oppressive 1960s/70s faculty buildings in the area. Obviously, dramatic changes had to occur to provide the research organisations with a presence on the campus, and the architects clearly enjoyed their task, but it was not all frivolous. The existing ground-floor uses of the building were to remain unaltered (and unaffected by building works), while the mezzanine level was to be converted to a separate floor providing offices, meeting facilities and two separate entries. To achieve this various structural acrobatics were required.

The Centres joins the Samuels Building (see page 164) in attempting to break new ground in architectural aesthetics at the university. However, the façades of this building are intentionally eclectic. New cladding on two façades becomes an undulating parapet disguising the existing saw-tooth roof. On the eastern façade a stuck-on layer of diagonally patterned cladding highlights the first floor, and the entrance is a tableau of colourful cut-outs. The abutting northern wall is rugged and functional with existing exposed brickwork, elliptical aluminium louvres and expressed roof plant. Nevertheless, the conjunction works.

ADDRESS University of NSW, Botany Street entrance, Randwick
CLIENT University of NSW
STRUCTURAL ENGINEER Structural Design Group
SIZE 1,260 square metres COST AUD$2.5 million
ACCESS to public areas

Eastern Suburbs

Campbell Luscombe Associates 1993

Campbell Luscombe Associates 1993

Quadrangle Building

The Quadrangle Building and the Quadrangle itself were conceived in the 1990 masterplan for the University of NSW. The 77 by 43-metre quadrangle is virtually at the centre of the campus at the eastern end of an axis which later became University Walk. Driven by guidelines which controlled the envelope, this building demonstrates the potential for both success and failure inherent in this method of design.

The three-storey building accommodates Student Union facilities, teaching space, offices and the Faculty of Commerce. Sophisticated and amenable, it extends around three sides of the quadrangle in a shallow U-shape and, with a projecting double-level colonnaded walkway and access through the building at several points, it fulfils the role of providing physical links to all parts of the campus. The building's long, curved, steel roof (the element which has almost become an architectural metaphor for Australian identity) is broken at the central entrance by a brick tower which, making references to Sir Edwin Lutyens in Delhi, adds to the strong colonial feel, but is awkwardly related to the body and rhythms of the building. At the south-western corner a rotunda-like cafeteria unexpectedly breaks out of the brick mass with a vitality that is lacking on the quadrangle side.

One cannot help thinking that an energetic burst through the building envelope and less concentration on the order of the façade would have created a more dynamic and significant building for this fulcrum site.

ADDRESS University of NSW Campus, Randwick
CLIENT University of NSW
STRUCTURAL ENGINEER Taylor Thomson Whitting
SIZE 18,000 square metres COST AUD$25 million
ACCESS to public areas

Eastern Suburbs

Peddle Thorp Architects 1993

Peddle Thorp Architects 1993

Wylie's Baths

Occupying both a special site in Sydney and a special place in the city's heart, Wylie's Baths have stood against the Coogee cliffs since 1907. Built by champion marathon swimmer H Alexander Wylie, they were instrumental in the development of Australian swimming, the venue for the first swimming championships in 1911, and one of the first mixed-bathing pools in the country.

The design was simple but spectacular vernacular architecture. A large, open, timber deck jutted from the crescent-shaped escarpment. Supported on a forest of hardwood posts it sat 7 metres above the 50-metre tidal pool, dug from a rock shelf and enclosed on the ocean side by concrete walls. Over the years several modifications were made, but in 1992 the platform was declared unsafe and condemned.

From an original brief for a new amenities block the architects persuaded their client to let them attempt to restore the spirit of the place. As one who learnt to swim there (as did the two designers) I can testify that they have succeeded. The new work is clearly modern, adding a layer to the rich history of the baths, but the concept remains. By careful examination and manipulation almost 80 per cent of the 174 support posts were retained, and the deck was rebuilt to its full 1929 extent, with some sections of the original remaining. New changing rooms were constructed, repeating the simple forms of the original with the addition of pyramid-shaped roofs and skylights over central solar-heated showers.

ADDRESS Neptune Street, Coogee
CLIENT Randwick Council
STRUCTURAL ENGINEER Miller Milston & Ferris
SIZE 780 square metres COST AUD$700,00
ACCESS open

Eastern Suburbs

Allen Jack + Cottier 1995

Allen Jack + Cottier 1995

South Sydney / Inner West

Allen Jack + Cottier Office Building

Set in Surry Hills, a somewhat dilapidated enclave near the centre of the city, this building, designed by the architects for themselves and another occupant, acts as a transition between the disparate types and scales of surrounding buildings – bulky brick warehouses, low-rise offices and lacy two-storey terrace houses. Visual unity in the area is brought about by the large number of brick buildings and the great variety of brick detailing they display. The architects, therefore, have designed a building that is modulated and animated by a rich vocabulary of detailing which weaves it into the streetscape and establishes an emphatic expression. Almost square in plan and occupying a complete block, its sculptural presence and classical composure bring a new sense of urbanity to the precinct. The banded brickwork is punctured by small square windows at the second-floor level, which cantilevers out over chopped-off corners and gives both movement and continuity to the façades. The brickwork stops above the two-storey entry, allowing the curved glass-block wall of the stairs to protrude. Recreation spaces on the roof are set back, forming a narrow enclosed strip along the middle of the building, which is read from the street as a graceful curve. Both these elements contrast with the otherwise orthogonal austerity of its form.

The building contains office accommodation on two levels, recreation facilities on the roof (including an open tennis court and terraces) and ground-floor parking for 36 cars.

ADDRESS 59 Buckingham Street, Surry Hills
CLIENT Allen Jack + Cottier/Ausminco Pty Ltd
STRUCTURAL ENGINEER Taylor Thomson Whitting
SIZE 3,385 square metres COST AUD$2.4 million
ACCESS on request

South Sydney / Inner West

Allen Jack + Cottier 1988

Allen Jack + Cottier 1988

Crown Street Housing

The entire 1-hectare site for this development was occupied by the Crown Street Women's Hospital from 1893 until its closure in 1983. Three of the original buildings remain. The project provides 236 one- and two-bedroom residential apartments and 3,500 square metres of commercial and retail space on two blocks in a run-down inner-city area which is becoming increasingly popular as an urban residential precinct. The design concept followed the guidelines prepared by the practice for the South Sydney Development Control Plan in 1989 – perimeter buildings with prominent corners and lower rows of infill terraces, street-defining walls and central open space (a fairly standard urban model for Europe but one that was not used in Sydney until the mid 1980s).

The northern block has three major components. Facing Crown Street is a flat seven-storey residential building with some retail and commercial uses and an original building adapted to commercial use. Apartment buildings front Riley, Albion and Fitzroy Streets, and the southern block is public housing in a mixture of four-storey walk-ups and two-storey infill row housing. Both sites have underground parking. The generous courtyards are lushly landscaped and contain two swimming pools.

Taking cues from the context as well as displaying influences from Rossi and Krier at IBA, this project reinforces and enriches the character and urban form of the area using a building type and plan form which provide a model for inner-city residential projects.

ADDRESS Crown, Albion and Riley Streets, Surry Hills
CLIENT Toga Building Company
STRUCTURAL ENGINEER MPN Group Consulting Engineers
COST AUD$70 million
ACCESS to courtyards

Travis McEwen Group 1993

Travis McEwen Group 1993

Powerhouse Museum

The museum gets it name from the original power station built on the 2.4-hectare site in 1899 to generate electricity for the city's tram system. When the trams stopped running in 1963, the building was closed and it remained vacant and decaying until the decision in 1979 for it to become the Museum of Applied Arts and Sciences. For 50 years this museum held 80 per cent of its collection in storage, including locomotives, aeroplanes, tramcars, and the 1795 Boulton and Watt steam engine. The new museum provides space for the permanent collection and for temporary and visiting exhibitions.

The walls and truss systems of the two cavernous brick buildings – the Boiler House and the Turbine Hall – were retained, and parallel to them on the west side two large arched structures were added, matching the original scale and providing contrasting dimensions of space and form. The tall, narrow atrium extending the full length of the site and the lower quadrant-shaped structure express themselves dramatically on Harris Street and generate the sensational progression of spaces that takes one through the building. From the entrance in the huge vaulted quadrant, down the series of zigzag ramps to the new galleria (which creates a top-lit shaft of space between the old and the new), through the sequence of brick arches to the immense spaces of the Turbine Hall and Boiler House, where buses and engines are dwarfed and real aeroplanes dangle from the ceilings, the building offers an experience as rewarding as the exhibits.

ADDRESS 500 Harris Street, Ultimo
CLIENT NSW Government, Museum of Applied Arts and Sciences
STRUCTURAL ENGINEER Bond James Laron Murtagh
SIZE 38,000 square metres COST AUD$97 million including fitout
ACCESS open Monday to Friday 9.00–17.00

NSW Government Architect 1988

NSW Government Architect 1988

ABC Radio and Orchestra Headquarters

When the Australian Broadcasting Corporation decided to unite the 12 radio stations which had been dispersed over Sydney for many years, one of the main requirements of the brief was to establish a corporate identity without losing each station's sense of individuality.

The architects proposed the structure of a township and the result is a complex of buildings fused into a whole around a 'town centre', a huge multi-level atrium running north–south along the middle of the site. On to the atrium face a ten-storey office block along the eastern side, a nine-storey tower for radio studios and recording halls at the northern end, and large recording halls to the south and west. The soaring atrium is a dynamic space. It generates all the circulation in the building and is alive with the rhythms and movement of a multiplicity of elements and structures that provide communication between floors – projecting flights of stairs, balconies, galleries and bridges. The saw-toothed, space-frame structure of its south-lit street-facing wall ends dramatically halfway down the vertical space, tying back across the atrium with slender steel struts and fanning out over the lounge area into a trussed, vaulted ceiling.

The town-centre concept also allowed the building an appropriate contextual scale, and a rich and intricate set of shapes and forms with which to interact in the heterogeneous environment of the street. The slim circular shaft on Harris Street is a fire stair and communications tower.

ADDRESS 700 Harris Street, Ultimo
CLIENT Australian Broadcasting Commission
STRUCTURAL ENGINEER Ove Arup & Partners
SIZE 43,000 square metres COST AUD$112 million
ACCESS to public areas

Anchor Mortlock & Woolley 1990

Anchor Mortlock & Woolley 1990

Faculty of Design, Architecture and Building

The six-level faculty building is the first stage of a complex which will eventually include a 16-level slab building at the rear of the site. Built to the street-line over a 130-vehicle car park, the new building is linear in plan and linked by a pedestrian bridge over Harris Street to other campus buildings. Reflecting the collegiate nature of a multi-disciplinary faculty, the plan is structured as a series of environments: the building is permeated by terraces and open space around which offices are grouped, in contrast to the usual shooting-gallery corridor configuration. On the main pedestrian level, the building form is opened up with two courtyards which allow fluid movement and easy contact between staff and students. A large daylit atrium space is the vertical focus, connecting the floors and doubling as the exhibition area for displays of students' work.

The building is also a 'living laboratory'. Building materials, technologies and services were designed to expose students and staff to a diverse range of solutions – including post-tensioned, band-beam, concrete-slab construction, conventionally reinforced flat plate and rib-slab, structural steel stairs, bowstring roof beams and the cable suspension structure of the footbridge.

The Harris Street façade is modelled in polished, precast-concrete cladding. Modern bay windows respond to nearby heritage façades, and a parasol-like curved roof creates a relationship with the ABC building.

ADDRESS University of Technology, 702–730 Harris Street, Ultimo
CLIENT University of Technology
STRUCTURAL ENGINEER Ove Arup & Partners
SIZE 16,300 square metres COST AUD$30 million
ACCESS open

Philip Cox Richardson Taylor & Partners 1994

Philip Cox Richardson Taylor & Partners 1994

Markets 3 Campus

As part of a strategy to enliven and rehabilitate areas of the inner city, the University of Technology (at that time the Institute of Technology) second campus was located in the former Fruit and Flower Markets Building (1911), part of the extensive markets precinct which was developed in the Haymarket by the City Council between 1909 and 1914, and vacated in the late 1970s when the markets were relocated. On a 1.2-hectare site bounded by four streets, the Markets 3 Campus building now accommodates the Information Resource Service, Faculty of Law, Faculty of Business Studies and Technical Teacher Training Division.

The original building featured an Italianate campanile and first-floor façades of banded brickwork and stone over roller-shuttered openings. The architects' decision to retain elements of this façade was a major determinant in the overall design, providing the visual framework from which new forms evolved. The campanile was retained, but separated from the building to form a stand-alone memory of the old market building and a major focal point for the campus. Key elements of the Quay Street façade were kept to form entranceways, gateways and screens, behind which rise the cubist shapes of the new campus. Clusters of different-sized building blocks, made all the more coherent by the consistent use of banded brickwork and the thematic repetition of key-hole openings, were carefully juxtaposed to create a visually dynamic sense of a city within a city, evoking tantalising memories of places Italian.

ADDRESS Quay Street, Haymarket
CLIENT University of Technology
STRUCTURAL ENGINEER Ove Arup & Partners
SIZE 20,000 square metres COST AUD$20.57 million
ACCESS open

Philip Cox Richardson Taylor & Partners 1986

Philip Cox Richardson Taylor & Partners 1986

Ansett Terminal, Sydney Airport

The Ansett Australia domestic terminal was fortuitously located in the right place for the airport's new third runway. This redevelopment doubled the terminal's capacity by extending the first finger and adding another one more or less parallel to it. It also included the construction of a new Golden Wing Lounge and a long, vaulted arcade linking the new ten-gate concourse to the main one.

The interiors of airport terminals are the parts that really matter: here the concourses and arcade are enlivened by roof lighting and gate lounges which open up with grand-piano-shaped, glazed curtain walls to the tarmac, allowing the aircraft to move in close. Major traffic nodes are marked by dramatic vertical drums, and at the elbow where the arcade stops and the gates start, there is an 11-metre-high, 20-metre-diameter, glass-domed nodal point supported on a spidery, bicycle wheel structure.

The entire steel-framed terminal is set on columns, putting embarking and disembarking passengers at the same height as the aircraft and creating a building which reads as a crisp white structure with elongated, elevated arms extending from the externally expressed circular forms of the nodes. The design of aerobridges and fire stairs as light, clip-on elements continues the same architectural vocabulary.

The Ansett Terminal had grown in an *ad hoc* fashion for many years; these additions have adroitly managed to give it visual and functional coherence.

ADDRESS Sydney Airport, Gardiners Road, Mascot
CLIENT Ansett Australia
STRUCTURAL ENGINEER Connell Wagner
SIZE 36,759 square metres COST AUD$34 million
ACCESS public

South Sydney / Inner West

Richard Fiala of Meldrum Burrows (now Humphrey Edwards) 1992

Richard Fiala of Meldrum Burrows (now Humphrey Edwards) 1992

International Terminal, Sydney Airport

The original International Terminal Building was designed by the Commonwealth Department of Works and altered in the 1980s to correct functional deficiencies in the design. This new wing, designed as an extension to the southern side of the building, was the first stage of development in the implementation of the 1988 masterplan which envisaged three new finger piers. Changing operational demands influenced the design of the new wing, with a long-span (15- by 12-metre grid), steel-frame structure to allow for easy modification and change of functions and activities. Arrivals and Departures remain on the existing lower and upper levels, but baggage collection is extended out under one of the upper roadways. The roadways are covered by a freestanding steel structure forming a long, curving, partly glazed roof, cantilevering 18 metres each side of central columns. Eventually these great flapping wings will extend along the front of the old building, unifying the terminal's appearance.

The problem of connecting the light, airy, spacious new interior with the drab, cramped old one was solved by placing a cruciform shopping arcade and food hall at the point where they meet. A high atrium separates this arcade from the check-in counters, behind which another high, daylit atrium runs the length of the building.

The concept behind the whole interior was to create a continuity of horizontal space and a sense of visual connection by using atriums, escalators, glazed lifts between floors and, where possible, natural lighting.

ADDRESS Sydney Airport, Gardiners Road, Mascot
CLIENT Federal Airport Corporation
STRUCTURAL ENGINEER Kinhill Engineers
SIZE 70,000 square metres COST AUD$240 million
ACCESS public

Stafford Moor & Farrington 1992

Stafford Moor & Farrington 1992

Waterloo Public Housing

This public housing project, part of a programme of regeneration by the Department of Housing in a rundown inner-city suburb (see also building opposite by Philip Cox, built to a similar brief), took the architectural tradition of the nineteenth-century street subdivision pattern as its design cue and foundation for an innovative scheme which provides for contemporary living requirements. A familiar row-housing rhythm is set up by elements of the façade, but this housing project is no historicist pastiche, and its planning offers a great deal more than the outdated nineteenth-century speculative terrace.

Thirty-two family and one-bedroom units are provided in a three-storey block, built to the street front of a long rectangular site. Sixteen family units, each using the whole of the ground floor and the rear of the upper two floors, have large courtyards at the back and individual entry from small front gardens. Sixteen one-bedroom units on the first and second floors, each with a central street-facing balcony, are entered by four sets of communal stairs. Light rolled-steel frames curve gracefully over back walls and gates to provide for many utilitarian uses.

The Walker Street façade is delicate and articulate. The slender steel columns supporting the round-ended balconies, the subtle vaulting of individual roofs projecting from the continuous lantern-like ridge, and the carefully considered detailing add to the 'livabilty' and elegance of this scheme, which creates a provocative model for urban housing.

ADDRESS 95–125 Walker Street, Waterloo
CLIENT NSW Department of Housing
STRUCTURAL ENGINEER Paterson Wholohan Grill
SIZE 3,120 square metres COST AUD$3.3 million
ACCESS none

South Sydney / Inner West

Peter Myers Architect 1992

Peter Myers Architect 1992

Faculty of Education

The new Sydney University building is located on a sloping site adjacent to a hockey field, called the Square. To the north is the Holmes Building, designed in the 1920s by Professor Leslie Wilkinson, Australia's first professor of architecture. To the south across the Square is his gracious Physics Building. Both were planned along an axis which passed through the Physics Building to St Paul's College further south. This axis had been ignored and forgotten, but was re-identified by University masterplanners Conybeare Morrison as the historic Wilkinson Axis. The Faculty of Education, which is built around this axis, unfortunately takes all its architectural cues not only from its neighbouring historic buildings, but from practically every period of architectural history. It is a *tour de force* of conceits and devices – striped Victorian brickwork, tiled friezes and chequerboard Dutch gables, large cornices, a corner drum-tower and bowed portico entry, gothic finials, Arts and Crafts pergolas, soldier-course window frames, and red Minoan and blue Doric columns. And if that were not enough, there are also references to Lutyens, Stirling and Jeremy Dixon, not to mention Venturi and Aldo Rossi.

It's all handled with a bold confidence, but even within the extraordinary parameters the architects have set, there are uncomfortable disparities of scale and proportion, and much of it reads as a collection of parts rather than an entity. Overall, it does not say much for confidence in modern architecture to fulfil the requirements of the University's brief.

ADDRESS The University of Sydney, Manning Road, Glebe
CLIENT The University of Sydney
STRUCTURAL ENGINEER Ove Arup & Partners
SIZE 11,000 square metres COST AUD$15 million
ACCESS open during university semesters

Jackson Teece Chesterman Willis 1995

Jackson Teece Chesterman Willis 1995

Leitch House

In 1979 Ed Lippmann worked with Marcel Breuer in New York in an environment which was 'infused with dedication, innovation and creativity'. It was a compelling experience for the young architecture student, whose work demonstrates his belief that 'the basic philosophy of the Bauhaus remains as fertile today as it was in the 1920s'. In this transformation of a late nineteenth-century, semi-detached, worker's cottage, he explores the principles of uniting art and industry, technology and humanity, with the added dimension of historical context.

The bay-windowed, porticoed and pedimented front façade of the original one-storey house remains, and around the corner, in the side street, the brick wall of the first two bedrooms is also intact. Beyond that, however, there is no further resemblance to a Victorian cottage. The building extends along the boundary of the site, taking advantage of the sloping land with an uncompromising two-storey steel and glass-block façade which fits under the simple pitched roofline of the front section.

The artist/client wanted light, open interiors. With a prefabricated steel structure which is both visually and structurally independent of the original brick building, the architect has created a flexible open space at the rear with living areas below and studio above. Steel-channel frames for the glass-block wall and the fully glazed two-storey end wall, floor and roof beams and the steel stairs, were all fabricated at the same time as the main frame, allowing steel assembly to take only three days and building completion four months.

ADDRESS 198 Young Street, Annandale
STRUCTURAL ENGINEER Fozzard Consulting Engineers
SIZE extension 120 square metres COST AUD\$176,000
ACCESS none

Lippmann Associates 1994

Lippmann Associates 1994

Ouzas House

This house explores a medium-cost alternative to the ubiquitous project house, which is invariably unsuitable for adaptation to specific site conditions. Built on a sloping site in a hybrid street in the fashionable inner-city suburb of Balmain, the split-level, strictly modern, steel and glass house sits into the terrain with its entrance and garage on street level. Above the garage the kitchen and family room open on to a front deck. Half a level up is the 4-metre-high living room, opening on to a large landscaped deck. A half level above this are two bedrooms and a bathroom.

The client budget dictated the need to do more with less, and a cost of AUD$900 per square metre was achieved by using standardised, mass-produced structural components, glazing, cladding and internal fitout systems which rely on off-site factory production rather than site-based wet trades. The lightweight steel-frame structure was made up of standardised elements, fabricated off-site and bolted together on site. The portal frames, internal walls and drop-in ceiling all conform to a 600-millimetre-square planning grid, and a 700-millimetre vertical module sets out the internal floors and mid levels. The building envelope is grey steel sheeting, which directs rainwater from a roll-curved external cornice. The wet service core is contained in a 2.4-metre spine.

Although the structural system is tightly controlled, the interior volumes are fluid and interconnecting, creating a rich spatial composition and a pavilion form which, glazed at the two frame ends, suggests further extensions of space.

ADDRESS 29 Rosser Street, Balmain
STRUCTURAL ENGINEER Fozzard Consulting Engineers
SIZE 98 square metres COST AUD$120,000
ACCESS none

Lippmann Associates 1995

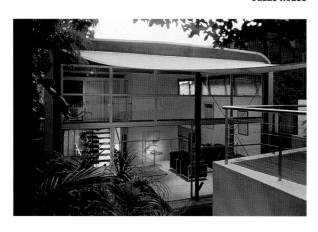

Lippmann Associates 1995

Meares House

Harry Seidler's latest house is a further development of his recent interest in the use of large multi-curved roofs covering whole buildings – as a means of exploiting and controlling space (see the Pittwater House, page 300) and creating volumes in which the roof contributes dynamically to the interaction of spaces. Externally, this house rolls down the hill to the harbour edge of its Balmain site in a series of great voluptuous waves, like the sea itself, or the visualisation of a piece of baroque music. The site, bounded on three of its sides by streets, a park and the harbour, is long and narrow, and is divided by the plan into three sections – a large entry courtyard at the rear of the site, with a double garage on the street and a store above; a two-storey split-level house (which itself is designed with three functional zones running across the site) with water-facing terraces; and a 15-metre swimming pool at the water's edge. The house is built to the street boundary, emerging as a contiguous part of the curving wall which runs the length of the site. Entry to the house is halfway along this wall.

The ground floor is planned with a central core containing the main entry, the stairs down to the living and dining area and their curvaceous terrace, the stairs up to the first-floor level, and the kitchen, bathrooms and utility rooms. A bedroom and study open on to the rear courtyard at this level. On the first floor is another study, in the central zone, which overlooks the entry space and leads on to a large, square terrace situated above the dining area. The main bedroom and dressing room face the rear courtyard, but the height of the entry/living space allows views from the bedroom to the harbour through a floor-to-ceiling glazed panel.

The complex, reverse-curve shapes of the roof were designed to interlock at their highest points over the entry and the first-floor study. The interlocking roofs create the main internal volume of space, which flows

Harry Seidler & Associates 1995

Harry Seidler & Associates 1995

from the entry to the living room and interacts with rooms and spaces on first-floor level. With their forms curving over the stretches of apparently seamless glass walls which face both the harbour and the garden courtyard, the roofs also create exciting visual relationships between the inside and outside of the house.

Materials are simple and long-lasting. The ground-floor finish is 610-by 1,060-millimetre, polished, precast-concrete paving blocks. The walls are split-face concrete blocks, ceilings are white-painted plasterboard and the roof is beige-coloured corrugated steel.

ADDRESS 22 White Street, Birchgrove
STRUCTURAL ENGINEER Birzulis Associates
SIZE 232 square metres COST AUD$550,000
ACCESS none

Harry Seidler & Associates 1995

Harry Seidler & Associates 1995

Glebe Island Bridge

While this bridge looks dramatic in photographs, it is actually the least attractive physical addition to Sydney since the Monorail (which can be easily dismantled), and it is difficult to understand how this city, which is normally so urban-design conscious, managed to let this gargantuan structure slip through the net with barely a murmur of protest. The 805-metre-long, concrete, cable-stayed bridge carries an arterial route across Johnstons Bay at Glebe Island and although, visually, it proclaims itself loudly all over the city as an important icon rivalling both the Opera House and the Harbour Bridge, its span is just 345 metres. The enormous height and omnipresence of the bridge would suggest that it is joining two areas separated by vast stretches of water, whereas prior to its construction one was barely aware that the old Glebe Island Bridge crossed any water at all. One can only view the new bridge with regret and think how wonderful a sleek, Calatrava-inspired structure would have looked in its place – leaping gracefully over the water, linking instead of separating the suburbs on either side.

The structure comprises three main spans of 140, 345 and 140 metres, which are cable-stayed and continuous, with three prestressed-concrete, twin box-girder end spans. The cable-stay section is supported by two semi-fan-shaped planes of stay cables. The delta-shaped reinforced-concrete towers are approximately 120 metres high with a maximum width of 44.23 metres. Each stay is individually anchored in a recess at the tower head and at a pod on the underside of the deck edge beams.

ADDRESS part of Glebe Island arterial route
STRUCTURAL ENGINEER Roads and Traffic Authority
LENGTH 805 metres COST AUD$90 million
ACCESS public motorway, cycleway and pedestrian way; no toll

Roads and Traffic Authority 1995

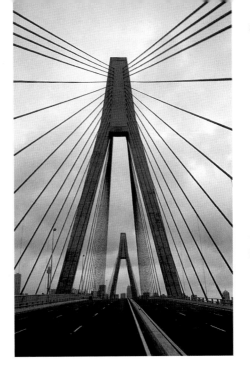

Roads and Traffic Authority 1995

Western / South-Western Suburbs

Australian Film, Television and Radio School

AFTRS is an independent statutory authority, established by the Federal Government in 1975 to provide training in writing, camera, sound editing, production management and direction for cinema, television and radio. The school is equipped with all the technical facilities of a modern production house, including three television studios, a radio station, drama studio, music studio, dubbing theatre and a 250-seat film theatre. The school is a dynamic body where the pattern of learning is both formal and informal, theoretical and practical, structured and unstructured. The one constant factor is change. The design concept was a metaphor for the school's requirement for a unique combination of creativity and imagination within an environment of elaborate and intricate technology.

The building links into two different planning grids. Set on the grid of Macquarie University, on whose campus it is located, it is bisected on the angle of the surrounding street pattern by an internal spine which progresses from the theatrical, proscenium-arched entrance, through the body of the building – assembling all the component elements and functions around it – to the movie-set gazebo at the other end. The gazebo projects into and overlooks the open valley of the university green belt. The various building elements are accommodated in arms which extend out from this spine, allowing for future expansion of individual departments if required.

The animated interior street, known as the 'Corso', provides contrast with the functional, introverted studios, articulates the importance of connections and communication between the activities and is a major activity area for the 200–300 staff and students. Social spaces are dispersed along the Corso, where electronic panels and video screens display information, and it overlooks a series of landscaped courtyards

Daryl Jackson Robin Dyke Pty Ltd 1988

Daryl Jackson Robin Dyke Pty Ltd 1988

on the eastern side, further adding to the sense of penetration into the labyrinth of facilities.

Immediately adjacent to the main entrance, on the eastern side, grouped around a centrally placed projection room, are the four theatres used to review and produce film material. Further along this side of the Corso the sound/radio production areas and studios are linked to the theatre and directors' suites. The west side of the Corso contains the three large sound-isolated studios and workshop areas. Three staircases along the spine provide a distribution of vertical access points.

The design concept for the structure was to provide a simple, two-storey, repetitive, reinforced-concrete frame to accommodate all the departments other than the studio and theatre blocks (which required double-volume height and large spans). As the architects intended, the building appears as a comprehensible assemblage of parts, with its elements expressed and distinguished in the manner of a small village, by mass and form rather than material. The roofs of the studio/theatres are expressed as bow-string or curved forms, facilitating rainwater run-off, structural spanning and air distribution principles. The lightweight, fibre cement skin is taut, banded and layered into its landscape setting with a solid cubist feel for mass.

ADDRESS Macquarie University Campus, Balaclava Road, North Ryde
CLIENT Australian Film, Television and Radio School
LANDSCAPE ARCHITECT Harry Howard & Associates
STRUCTURAL ENGINEER Ove Arup & Partners
SIZE 10,000 square metres COST AUD$18 million
ACCESS open

Daryl Jackson Robin Dyke Pty Ltd 1988

Daryl Jackson Robin Dyke Pty Ltd 1988

Sydney International Athletics Centre

When this stadium and the nearby Aquatic Centre were designed and built, the site for the 2000 Olympics was little more than a vast 760-hectare, derelict landscape of cleared stockyards and industrial sites. This presented a challenging design problem, made more difficult by the fluctuating constraints and indecisions of a volatile masterplan. Nevertheless, the design of these two buildings has cleverly related them to the undulating expanses of the topography and provided a strong architectural language on which the Olympic city and the future sports-oriented urban centre can build.

For the Olympics, this modest but elegant stadium, linked by a tunnel for competitors to the main stadium, will function as the warm-up track for the athletics and field events. The curving grandstand is designed as an extension of a series of earth berms which define the arena and provide grass seating (or a base for 10,000 temporary seats) and wind protection for the track. Roads and concourses are designed to respond to the mounded earth forms, and paved areas wind between various sections, enhancing the spectator's sense of sitting in the landscape.

The 150-metre gently arched roof, suspended by a network of cables from two 45-metre-high masts, tilts forward to cover approximately half the seated spectators. A catenary cable curved over the entire roof length provides resistance from uplift forces, and a flaring, steel-skirt, truss beam encircles and supports the seating from behind.

ADDRESS Sydney Olympics Park, Homebush
CLIENT NSW Public Works Department
STRUCTURAL ENGINEER Connell Wagner
SIZE 8,500 square metres COST AUD$23 million
ACCESS public

Philip Cox Richardson Taylor/Peddle Thorp Architects 1993

Philip Cox Richardson Taylor/Peddle Thorp Architects 1993

Sydney International Aquatic Centre

This multi-functional swimming complex was the result of a government initiative to provide NSW with a new Olympic swimming venue and support for Sydney's bid for the 2000 Olympics. The centre comprises a collection of pools, ranging from the strictly serious Olympic variety to a free-form fun model with all the trimmings, plus gymnasium, aerobics room, saunas, café and 4,400 permanent spectator seats for the competition pools, which can be extended to 12,500 during the Games.

The Aquatic Centre is planned on a circle with a radius of 102.5 metres. Half the circle is taken up by the building, the other half is a public recreation garden. Like the Athletics Centre, it is integrated with the form of the surrounding landscape, and the high earth berm which wraps around to the south and east reduces the impact of the 18.5-metre roofline and allows a low, enclosing, vaulted-entry subway – a dramatically contrasting arrival to the spaciousness and light of the interior. However, both the berm and the 135-metre-long arched steel transfer truss (a major element, structurally and visually, of the building) have another significant function, which was a driving consideration in the design. The truss supports the roof along its eastern edge, allowing the additional Olympic seating (after removal of the existing wall) to extend up the earth bank. After the Olympics, the seating will be removed and the building will return to its normal state. Unlike some Olympic megastructures, there will be no curtained-off areas of dead space in this venue.

Beyond the tunnel and past the reception desk is the concourse, a bridge which gives a sweeping overview of the whole expansive complex. From here the various elements and the structure and activity of the centre can all be seen. To the left are the competition diving and swimming pools, set in an ordered and functional surround of steeply-raked seating tiers under a steel-gridded, arched roof. To the right stretches an entirely

Philip Cox Richardson Taylor/Peddle Thorp Architects 1994

Philip Cox Richardson Taylor/Peddle Thorp Architects 1994

different panorama, and one of joyful informality: two leisure pools, arranged with lavish amounts of space between and around them for those who don't want to get wet. Here an island with imitation beach and real palm trees, a curvy pool with a 'rock pool' mosaic-tile floor designed by Sydney artist Colin Lancely, spiralling slides, frothing fountains, arched bridges, snaking seating and a glass wall with sunlight beaming through, set the scene for the serious activity of having fun in the water. Straight ahead are the 'outdoor' cafés, gyms and other facilities, and beyond the glazed end wall is the lushly landscaped sun-garden.

Structural steel was used extensively as the principal support framing for the building's superstructure. The competition hall structure is a tied arch form with a wide-span, steel diagrid frame consisting of a diagonal network of steel tubes which allow a column-free space for viewing. The leisure area, however, was constructed using internal columns and a roof supported by a series of cable trusses.

Both the interior and exterior of the building offer many visual rewards, but some of the external forms, after the strength of the earth mound, the huge arched truss and the curving glass wall around the leisure section, become less coherent as they approach the diameter of the circle. The embracing forecourt area to the entry subway, however, is a small triumph; it creates a real 'sense of place' in a landscape that is, at the time of writing, a barren wilderness. Take your togs.

ADDRESS Sydney Olympics Park, Homebush
CLIENT NSW Public Works Department
STRUCTURAL ENGINEER Connell Wagner
SIZE 14,500 square metres COST AUD\$65 million
ACCESS public

Philip Cox Richardson Taylor/Peddle Thorp Architects 1994

Western / South-Western Suburbs

Philip Cox Richardson Taylor/Peddle Thorp Architects 1994

Children's Medical Research Institute

The Children's Medical Research Institute is not one of the most exciting buildings by this respected architectural practice. Well planned, well mannered, refined, functional, and built to a low budget with simple materials and structural system, it fails to thrill, or even more than mildly interest the onlooker. With the majority of the floor space taken up by research laboratories requiring clinical isolation and environmental control, it is not a building for the public. This aloofness is reflected in the façade, which is bland and inexpressive despite the geometry of the plan, the setback ground floor, the sun-louvred first floor and the imagery of the sloping steel roofs. However, the Institute contains many close research links with the New Children's Hospital (see page 224) and is located on the same campus, defining the southern side of the entry fore-court. While being functionally and financially independent of the hospital, to a certain extent it reads as part of that complex.

Planned over two levels, the building contains administration, directorate, stores and a library at ground level and 12 laboratory spaces on the first floor. The plan form, with a central core of support areas surrounded by groups of four laboratories in a pinwheel configuration, facilitates the addition of a further four laboratories (without disrupting the functioning of the building) and provides for a link to the new hospital. There is a quadrant-shaped atrium at the centre of the plan with an access stair which is a focal and orientational element within its symmetry.

ADDRESS Hawkesbury Road, Westmead
CLIENT Children's Medical Research Institute
STRUCTURAL ENGINEER Ove Arup & Partners
SIZE 4,500 square metres COST AUD$12 million
ACCESS none

Anchor Mortlock & Woolley 1992

Anchor Mortlock & Woolley 1992

New Children's Hospital

This very special New Children's Hospital, in the demographic centre of Sydney, replaces its inner-city, turn-of-the-century predecessor and sets a new design programme and civic approach for a large hospital building. A specialised teaching hospital of the University of Sydney, associated with the Children's Medical Research Institute, it handles the most serious childhood ailments, from major accidents to diseases such as leukaemia. It is sited on 11 hectares of land, and its 75,000 square metres (the equivalent of a 60-storey office tower) are contained in a building with a footprint of approximately 2 hectares. With more than 2,000 staff, plus patients and visitors, the hospital is like a small city, and its planning was based on a strong urban concept and ideas which were radical in hospital design in Australia.

The process began with the client's request that the new building should not look institutional (like Westmead Hospital, the 1970s megastructure a little further up Hawkesbury Road) and that its design should be particularly responsive to the needs and welfare of children. The 1990 masterplan by State Projects, an arm of NSW Public Works, emphasised that the building should have an appropriate scale and environment for children and families. As summed up by one medico, the complex building programme called for 'a workspace for various healthcare and other professionals, a hotel for its guests (with all the associated infrastructure of communal life), a local and regional institution and an icon symbolic of humanist healthcare philosophy'.

To counteract the usual totalitarian hospital image, State Projects divided the masterplan into four distinct parts – Outpatients, Clinical Services, Wards and the Main Building. Four different design teams were selected to carry out the work, making it difficult to decide if this is actually one building or four. In a complete turnabout of the usual urban

Various architects 1995

Various architects 1995

design procedure, and contradicting the notion of urban rules and common language, each architect was encouraged to be different, and to negotiate outcomes evolving from the richness and complexity of inter-action during the design process.

Designed to recreate the dynamics of a village, the entire complex is arranged around four elements – the two major spaces (the entrance court at the corner of Hawkesbury Road and the children's garden which faces the Parramatta River) and the two main organising spines linking them (the glass-roofed galleria and the long north–south courtyard). The uniting of these distinct and individually designed structures (via shared arteries) has created a building which reads as a vibrant composition of shapes and forms rather than a static, monolithic shell. It also enables the business of the hospital to be carried out efficiently within spaces that are playful and interesting rather than intimidating. The massive bulk of the structure is never apparent.

A strong sense of place is created by the forecourt, which is defined by the forms of the Main Building and the Outpatients Department. Although by far the most dominant buildings in the whole complex – and the only two which can be seen on arrival – they are carefully scaled and shaped to create a lively, friendly and identifying image.

From the forecourt visitors are funnelled towards the wavy glass entrance canopy and into the Main Building, designed by Lawrence Nield & Partners. This building contains admissions and discharge, diagnostic and treatment areas, operating theatres, retail and coffee shops, dining and restaurant facilities, educational and conference areas and the galleria – the spine which gives legibility to the whole complex. Stepping back in a series of layers, with a long, undulating roof which serves as a dramatic backdrop and integrates the complex, the scale of the structure

Various architects 1995

Various architects 1995

is successfully mitigated into a form which Lawrence Nield describes as 'a village in front of a mountain'. The building also projects a comforting message of state-of-the-art technology to patients, families and visitors.

Separated from it by a long, narrow courtyard (built, surprisingly, in the style of a mountain-gorge, Chinese landscape) and linked to it by three glass overhead bridges, is the large Clinical Services Building by Woods Bagot. This, the most technically daunting and least public part of the hospital, is a more serious, straightforward complex, with overtones of international modernism bursting into colourful Mondrian-like gridded screens on the exterior. It provides a strong, compositional element in the development, but has responded in a less innovative way to the programme than the other buildings.

The Outpatients Department by McConnell Smith & Johnson employs yet another architectural language, using bold colour to re-inforce and subdivide its cubic forms and modulate its scale. A covered way, conveying a sense of landscape, overlays the exterior with a touch of whimsy. The building is entered from the main galleria and its circulation spine, which continues the landscape theme with strong earthy colours and randomly raked steel poles (suggesting a built forest) supporting a canopy of elliptical shapes. This helps to reduce the apparent length of the circulation path and defines a series of clearings within it. Waiting rooms are organised around landscaped courtyards which penetrate deeply into the otherwise solid block.

On the east–west axis, at the end of the galleria, is the Wards Building by Healthworks, the State Projects architects. In a faceted U-shape, the wards establish the edge of the second important landscape area of the site, the children's gardens. Here the formality of the landscape design and architecture is fragmented and softened by the patterns and colours

Various architects 1995

of the brick, glass and steel structures, and their volumes and surfaces, made sculptural by projecting balconies and sail-like awnings, create an almost tropical-resort feel. Despite this careful consideration and the undoubted attention to detail in the wards themselves, this section of the complex seems strangely at odds with the rest and is a rather unsatisfying and abrupt ending to the fascinating journey through the complexities of the light-filled galleria. A more pronounced transition space between the two might have resolved the problem.

Doctors and staff, patients and families, have been wholeheartedly enthusiastic about the building, which was completed on time and well under budget. It is ironic that it is only the architectural critics who have expressed reservations. While acknowledging and commending the intention of the programme, the overall success and the many delightful aspects of the development, the consensus opinion suggests greater dialogue between the designers and more control by the masterplanners would have resulted in an even more successful scheme.

ADDRESS Hawkesbury Road, Westmead
CLIENT NSW Department of Health and Royal Alexandra Hospital for Children
ARCHITECTS Main Building – Lawrence Nield & Partners;
Clinical Services Building – Woods Bagot;
Outpatients Department – McConnell Smith & Johnson;
Wards Building – Healthworks
STRUCTURAL ENGINEERS Taylor Thomson Whitting; Maunsell;
Ove Arup & Partners; State Projects
SIZE 75,000 square metres COST AUD$318 million
ACCESS to public areas

Various architects 1995

Various architects 1995

School of Industrial and Graphic Design

The University of Western Sydney, established in 1989, is based on the University of California model. With three independent network members, each containing several campuses, university education is reaching deep into Sydney's far-flung Western Suburbs, previously served only by technical colleges. The Penrith campus occupies an enormous area of 148 hectares. The Werrington South site is the least developed of the three that make up the campus. Its few buildings appear isolated and out of place in the rolling stretch of treeless countryside which, at this stage, shows not the slightest suggestion of the pedestrian precinct which will link the facilities, or of the other refinements which are planned.

The School of Design is a simple rectangular block of two and three storeys, cut through with a wide, top-lit gallery which splays out from the entrance, forming the access through the building and the central meeting place. Water from the roof runs down the three floors of the building through an elaborate down-pipe (a combination of fountains and spouts) into a free-form pool/seating arrangement in the gallery space. The architect intended that the building should appear as a series of shed forms in the landscape, an imagery achieved by a variety of sloping roofs and the corrugated-metal cladding used on both walls and roofs. A wide arch, cut out of a solid concrete screen wall set independently and at an angle to the building, proclaims its identity as a school of design.

ADDRESS University of Western Sydney, O'Connell Street, Werrington, Nepean
CLIENT University of Western Sydney
STRUCTURAL ENGINEER Low & Hooke
SIZE 4,460 square metres COST AUD$5.8 million
ACCESS open

Suters Architects Snell 1994

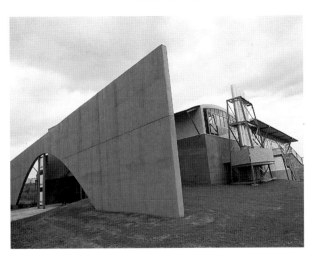

Suters Architects Snell 1994

John and Patricia Ward Library

The immensely sophisticated Ward Library, sitting alone and unconnected on top of the highest point of the barren Werrington South Campus, could easily have been designed for an Oxbridge site. Built around a high and narrow central spine which dramatically slices the length of the structure, giving framed vistas to the rolling hills at either end, this building has clarity and complexity. Nevertheless, it challenges the vast expanses of the campus with the power of its uncompromisingly directional and strongly delineated forms (their starkness subtly subdued by pink brickwork and render), which signal a relationship with the university site across the highway and give an indication of the proposed urbanity of the as yet unrealised campus.

The central spine divides the library functionally and accommodates both vertical and horizontal circulation with a series of stairs, lifts, and bridge crossings on the upper floors. On the eastern side, a two-storey section, swooping out from the two high walls which sandwich the central spine, contains the reference desks, catalogues, reference and slide collections. The three-storey western side, containing the main book collection and study carrels, is long and straight, expressing the rhythm of seven individually articulated bays with gently arched roofs.

Another interesting library by the same architect can be seen on the neighbouring Kingswood site of this campus.

ADDRESS The University of Western Sydney, O'Connell Street, Werrington, Nepean
CLIENT University of Western Sydney
STRUCTURAL ENGINEER Miller Milston & Ferris
SIZE 6,000 square metres COST AUD$8.4 million
ACCESS open

Bruce James & Partners 1993

Bruce James & Partners 1993

Penrith Civic Centre

Penrith, 50 kilometres due west of central Sydney, is the centre of the fastest growing suburban district in the metropolitan area. Penrith Council's staff were previously housed in five different buildings, and this site had been ear-marked for a new Civic Centre since the early 1980s. The architect for this project, who runs a very small practice, won the commission from a group of seven other architects which included most of the city's heavyweights. His collaboration with the Council in this formidably conservative area has been described as 'an oddly successful marriage of Lone Ranger Architect and Brave New World Council'.

The Council's intention was to create a new civic focus on the site (at the western end of the city's existing centre) comprising cultural, commercial and civic facilities. To this end, the Joan Sutherland Performing Arts Centre (see page 240) was built on the south-west side of the site with partial Council funding in 1989. In 1994 Penrith Plaza Shopping Mall (see page 242), which involved complex land swaps with the Council, was also completed. Unfortunately, they were both designed and built on this one city block without input from a detailed masterplan.

The architect's interpretation of Council's brief was that it should have a powerful presence; be friendly, welcoming and democratic; provide Penrith with a new image, and bring the two very disparate neighbouring buildings into a coherent civic relationship. The resulting building certainly has presence. On the southern side two great ramped arms swoop out on either side of the circular entry in a way that is embracing and at the same time somewhat menacing (not to mention reminiscent of Romaldo Guirgola's Parliament House in Canberra). The Council Chambers sit on top of the entry. The plan is centrifugally dynamic, and the whole building is dramatically volatile with spatial tensions and juxtapositions combined with a kind of 'laid-back' energy.

Feiko Bouman Architect 1994

Feiko Bouman Architect 1994

Council offices and staff/public meeting rooms hook in a large curve around an axial light-flooded atrium which, running at right angles to the entry, is the public's one-stop shop, its point of contact with the Council. If open planning denotes being democratic, the building has certainly achieved that status. Staff circulation routes on the first floor take place on a mezzanine level visible from the atrium, and on the ground floor the atrium itself is the main circulation spine for staff. It's an easy walk up the stairs off the atrium to the mezzanine and to the centrally located Council Chambers. The Library is contained on the ground floor in a large triangular space. Its southern face runs on a 45-degree axis through the centre of the entry and its eastern face abuts the Penrith Plaza building.

While there is some lack of discipline in this building, particularly if you look closely at the detailing, its sprawling, organic gestural plan and its confident translation into three dimensions give it a quality which is particularly suited to this site on the flat plains at the foothills of the Blue Mountains.

What could have been a meaningful civic open space – and a grander setting for the building – has been mostly given over to a public car park.

Don't forget to look at the roofscape – perhaps the best view of all.

ADDRESS 601 High Street, Penrith
CLIENT Penrith City Council
STRUCTURAL ENGINEER Birzulis Associates
SIZE 5,000 square metres COST AUD$24 million
ACCESS to public areas

Feiko Bouman Architect 1994

Feiko Bouman Architect 1994

Joan Sutherland Performing Arts Centre

The Dame, as it is affectionately called by the locals, was the first of the trio of buildings on the site of the new Penrith Civic Centre, and was considered by Penrith Council to be the catalyst for the whole complex. In design terms, the Performing Arts Centre had three significant urban roles to play: to express Penrith's emerging identity, to create a general vocabulary that could be unspecifically adapted to future buildings on the site, and to be expressive of its theatrical and public purpose.

With long, curving corrugated-metal roofs floating above expanses of glass, the building sits easily in the flat landscape, and its form echoes the rolling foothills of the Blue Mountains. It is a simple and graceful building, effortlessly expressing the poetry and rhythms of dance and music. But with its architectural language more lyrical than civic, the Centre is somewhat at odds with the more overt forms of the Council Offices (see page 236), which express an entirely different functional programme.

The Centre accommodates 580 people in the main auditorium, which is designed as a traditional, box-shaped music hall with fine exposed bow-trusses and a surrounding colonnaded gallery. Other functions contrast as dynamic spaces around the hall. The main foyer is high and glazed all round, with a mezzanine level emerging from the auditorium.

The building, angled towards the civic centre and public open space, is also used as a venue for exhibitions, displays and teaching.

ADDRESS Henry Street, Penrith
CLIENT Penrith City Council
STRUCTURAL ENGINEER Ove Arup & Partners
SIZE 5,000 square metres COST AUD$6 million
ACCESS open

Philip Cox Richardson Taylor & Partners 1990

Philip Cox Richardson Taylor & Partners 1990

Penrith Plaza

Unlike in the US and the UK, where covered regional shopping centres are generally situated on vast sites in the midst of acres of car parking, in Sydney, which has a tradition of Victorian through-block arcades to build on, these megalithic structures have been more usually integrated with the existing town-centre fabric, with their parking contained in purpose-designed buildings. While never the greatest feats of architecture, these shopping centres have often been the catalyst for the regeneration and growth of a town or suburb, rather than the cause of its demise. This vast new complex, one of the largest in Australia, is by all indications one of the major factors contributing to Penrith Council's hopes and plans for a great spurt in business sector growth and the physical transformation of the area into a thriving regional metropolis.

The Lend Lease Corporation, the deliverer of this modern miracle, is a large, extremely successful organisation which, since 1951, has been involved in design, development, financing, project management and construction of an ever-increasing variety of projects. As early as the 1960s and 70s, it was responsible for the development of two major Sydney landmarks, Australia Square and MLC Tower (for which Harry Seidler was architect). With Penrith Council's decision to establish a new civic focus on a site to the immediate west of the old town centre (see two previous entries), Lend Lease took the opportunity to become part of the venture by extending and transforming its adjacent 1970s shopping mall into this new centre. Without breaking any new ground architecturally, Penrith Plaza has rethought and refined the pattern and greatly extended the programme of this building type.

Penrith Plaza doesn't aim to confuse and bombard the senses with a disorienting circulation pattern, gaudy colours and blaring music. Rather, it has returned to the mode (but not the decorum) of the decorated cast-

Lend Lease Design Group 1994

Lend Lease Design Group 1994

iron Victorian arcade, an elongated, light-filled galleria with mezzanine and transepts, and long promenades interrupted only with places to stop and browse, talk, eat and drink. In short, this is suburban Sydney's answer to the Roman Forum and the Champs Elysées, wrapped up in the exuberant glitz and glamour of a Busby Berkeley movie set. Even though you might pine for the elegance and restraint of the Milan Galleria, you would have to admit that the Plaza has become the spot in Penrith to peruse, perambulate, take coffee and, perhaps, even pontificate.

Reconstruction of the former mall has tripled its size. There are 220 retail outlets and parking for 3,000 cars, in two six-storey buildings on a site covering 63,000 square metres. The monumental glass-roofed arcade runs parallel to Penrith's main street and is over 300 metres long. The impact of the mall's enormous length is relieved by a series of secondary spaces forming three cross-malls, which effectively establish the building's precincts. Linear progression is also punctuated by a series of courtyard spaces.

The central court is the main feature of the galleria. Topped with a glittering dome, it is not only the heart of the mall but also, despite the Council's best intentions to create a civic space associated with its own new building, the real heart of the whole civic complex. The mall has a busy but delicate filigree appearance, created by the combination of patterns of the white-painted steel trusses, arches and ribs, the fine steel mullions silhouetted against the sky, and the sparkling, elaborate decoration of the arches, column capitals and domes.

The exterior of the building is less successful. The huge site is bounded by three main streets and although there has been a serious attempt to move away from the blank façades typical of such developments – by using good quality materials and by introducing variety (in the expression

Lend Lease Design Group 1994

of detail, columns and grid patterns) and civic gestures (glazed awnings, colonnades, shop windows, and a couple of eye-catching glazed entries) – as street architecture it is rather confused and suburban and expresses its overriding commercial programme far more strongly than a civic design agenda.

The Plaza's links with the so-called spaces of the civic centre are tenuous to say the least. A detailed masterplan for the whole civic area was a necessary prerequisite if the civic precinct were to achieve the results the Council so obviously desired. Unfortunately no such plan existed.

Western / South-Western Suburbs

ADDRESS Henry Street, Penrith
CLIENT Lend Lease General Property Trust and ANZ Bank
STRUCTURAL ENGINEER Lend Lease Design Group
SIZE 63,000 square metres COST AUD$250 million
ACCESS open

Lend Lease Design Group 1994

Lend Lease Design Group 1994

Sydney International Regatta Centre

The Finishing Tower is the largest of several structures designed by the architects for the 2000 Olympics canoeing and rowing events. To a masterplan by Context, the landscape arm of Conybeare Morrison & Partners, the tower is built on one of the lakes created by the Penrith Lakes Development Corporation as part of a programme to convert disused quarries into recreational facilities.

Tall and slender, the tower is built out over the water, with a top viewing balcony for the 'finish' camera and a large sheltering roof which presents its back to the northerly sun and winds. It has stepped seating for the judges watching the finishing line, spaces for administration and a good deal of electronic equipment. The curved form of the roof allows a string of solar panels along its edge to face the sun at an efficient angle. In an experiment to gauge efficiency and set the standard for larger energy-saving projects (to be developed when the grandstand is built), solar power will pass straight into the power grid to be used by the recreational facilities when in operation, or the local community at other times.

The northern lakeside has a string of small huts at intervals along the course for timing and short race starting. Together with the mobile starting tower, they form a family of structures similar in form, construction and materials to the Finishing Tower. With their feet in the water, they all engage in a reflective dialogue with the shimmering lake.

ADDRESS north side of Castlereagh Road between Leland Street and Sheens Lane, Penrith
CLIENT Olympic Coordination Authority
STRUCTURAL ENGINEER Northrop Holmes Consulting Engineers
SIZE 272 square metres COST AUD$1.05 million including site works
ACCESS open

Conybeare Morrison & Partners 1996

Conybeare Morrison & Partners 1996

Fairfax Printing Works

Fairfax, the publishers of the *Sydney Morning Herald* and the *Australian Financial Review*, required their new plant to be in operation within two years of their decision to move from the inner-city building which had housed their printing and editorial divisions for over 50 years but was by the 1990s unsuitable for modern newspaper production. Initially, Lend Lease considered ten different areas and more than 50 potential sites. The 10.2-hectare Chullora site was selected for its proximity to the demographic centre of Sydney and its excellent rail and road links.

The new rectangular building, five times larger than the *Financial Times* printing works in London, is really a giant shed with a series of vast corrugated-steel roofs stretching over enormous floor spaces and huge panels of glazing. On the eastern, highway façade, the fully glazed press hall pushes vertically through the building, breaking the line of the sweeping expanse of roof which tucks into the hilly ground at the southern end of the site and forms a covered dispatch area. The press hall displays the AUD$100-million machinery which is the *raison d'être* of the building. Through an internal viewing window near the entrance, the laser-guided robots serving the machinery can be viewed.

A defining factor of the programme was the client's desire to eliminate physical and visual barriers between different sections of the operation. This has resulted in a remarkable internal openness.

ADDRESS Hume Highway, Chullora
CLIENT John Fairfax Holdings
STRUCTURAL ENGINEER Lend Lease Design Group
SIZE 38,000 square metres
COST total AUD$300 million; design and construction AUD$84 million
ACCESS to public viewing areas and museum

Western / South-Western Suburbs

Lend Lease Design Group 1995

Lend Lease Design Group 1995

Macquarie Street, Liverpool

Although Liverpool, the first town established by colonial Governor Macquarie, was set out with a main street which was 30 per cent wider than usual, and contained a charming Francis Greenway church, by the late 1980s it had long since lost its historic charm and country town atmosphere. This urban design project has transformed two blocks of a typically bleak, suburban main street into a lively boulevard. With the complete pedestrianisation of one of the blocks, a public space was also created that is already performing as a vibrant town centre for the community. As part of the redevelopment of the Central Business District, the Liverpool City Council financed the improvements to Macquarie Street with the profits from the sale of a section of the street (at its northern end) to one of Sydney's major retail developers. A large shopping centre now closes the vista along the boulevard.

The 250-metre-long pedestrian mall continues the new boulevard treatment of the open section of street and reinforces the Macquarie Street axis. Regularly spaced mature trees and the elegant, curving lights which hang high over the street space, give a rhythmic sense of arching along the mall's full length. This rhythm and coherence are emphasised by a series of structures, shaped from various curving forms, which straddle or sit in the street space at irregular intervals, creating a sequence of places of distinct character and function and providing shaded and sheltered seating. The gently arching pergola structure has electronically controlled louvres which vary the amount of sunlight on the area and automatically close in the rain. The mall design also includes a civic square, a stage and performance area, lawns and terraced spaces, a giant chessboard, a fountain, cafés and seating.

Community consultation was a significant aspect of the project. Traffic, parking, and the pedestrianisation of Macquarie Street were all

Conybeare Morrison & Partners 1994

Conybeare Morrison & Partners 1994

matters of concern to the community and were opened up to public debate before any firm decisions were made. Five competition concept schemes were also exhibited to stimulate ideas and discussions within the community. The architects' final plan incorporated many of the community suggestions and, similarly, many of the artworks in the mall resulted from interaction between council, artists, architects, shopkeepers, community groups and residents.

This is an interesting example of how the facilities and attractions provided by a huge covered shopping centre in a suburban main street can upgrade the image and amenity of the area and contribute to a town's prosperity. In this case, the upgraded street (which has also become the catalyst for the transformation of other streets in the vicinity) is fast becoming the setting for other types of commercial activity and now offers experiences which are different yet complementary to the intense shopping activity of the covered plaza.

The open mall and the covered giant plaza, so often seen as bitter enemies, may yet turn out to be a winning team. Certainly, the citizens of Liverpool have benefited greatly.

ADDRESS Macquarie Street, Liverpool
CLIENT Liverpool City Council
STRUCTURAL ENGINEER Northrop Holmes Consulting Engineers
SIZE 450 metres COST AUD$4 million
ACCESS open

Conybeare Morrison & Partners 1994

Western / South-Western Suburbs

Conybeare Morrison & Partners 1994

Northern Suburbs

Glen Street Offices and Apartments

The original six-storey office building which stands on this site, at the top of a sandstone cliff overlooking Sydney Harbour, was designed by Harry Seidler (and includes the architect's own offices on the top floor) and built in 1973. These additions, each a separate office building, were carried out in two stages, continuing the existing building's architectural character and use of materials. The old and new form a cohesive whole and a dramatic stretch of urban streetscape. However, certain factors – an irregularly shaped allotment, altered building laws, and a requirement that a proportion of the development be residential – contributed to subtle differences in form and structure. Whereas the original building is rectilinear with repetitive precast-concrete T-beam floors, the additions have some irregular, curvilinear walls of prestressed concrete poured *in-situ* into flowing horizontal and vertical curve and counter-curve elements.

In the first addition, the new office floors have three spans, with a central core on the street side and continuous sunshading terraces facing the harbour view. The two top floors accommodate a penthouse apartment which, although independently accessible from the new lift core, is connected to the architect's office with a theatre/exhibition space on the fifth floor. Entry to the apartment is breathtaking – directly into the two-storey-high reception and dining area, which has a panoramic water view stretching out beyond the long, fully glazed wall. The half-elliptical, polished-granite dining table is designed to allow guests to sit around the curved side facing the view. A sensuous winding stair leads to the upper-floor lounge area, study and master bedroom suite.

The free-flowing curves of the seamless, double-height wall and the glass balustrade of the terrace enrich the spatially open interiors. They also allow the building to become part of the curving shape of the bay, and visually connect it with the sweep of the Harbour Bridge (which can

Harry Seidler & Associates 1988, 1994

Harry Seidler & Associates 1988, 1994

be seen from the terrace), creating the impression that the building is an intrinsic part of an encircling swoop of physical form, both natural and man-made, surrounding that part of the harbour and continuing to Walsh Bay and beyond.

Materials and furniture have been chosen for their everlasting quality. The apartment floor is paved in grey Sardinian granite slabs, which are also used on the kitchen and bathroom walls and floors. The dining table, stair treads and all horizontal furniture tops are of exotic Indian Tamin granite. Only the artworks (by Frank Stella, Josef Albers, and Roy Lichtenstein amongst others) are colourful, in contrast to the neutral grey, white and black interior furnishings. As the architect says, 'nothing in the interiors should ever be in need of change'.

The second part of the addition, five floors high, continues the curve on the western wall but returns to rectilinear geometry on the street side to end the building. It adds a further subtle complexity to the articulation of the street façade by setting back its top three floors, thereby mediating between the planar differences of the other two sections.

The one-storey apartment on the fifth floor continues the same palette of materials, and shares a centrally located terrace with its neighbour.

ADDRESS 2A and 4 Glen Street, Milsons Point
CLIENT Contec Properties Pty Ltd
STRUCTURAL ENGINEER Birzulis Associates
SIZE no. 2A: offices – 1,010 square metres, apartment – 413 square metres, terraces – 351 square metres; no. 4: offices – 1,294 square metres, apartment – 144 square metres, terraces – 310 square metres
COST no. 2A: AUD$2.7 million; no. 4: AUD$2.5 million
ACCESS none

Harry Seidler & Associates 1988, 1994

Harry Seidler & Associates 1988, 1994

Stanton Library & Commercial Offices

North Sydney Council was able to create a new public open space by rationalising the use of its 2-hectare site, much of which was surface car park. By putting the parking in a two-storey building on one edge of the site, the architect created sufficient space for a new commercial office building (incorporating the existing Stanton Library) and a park with a grassy amphitheatre. The refurbishment of the library, which will eventually expand into the ground and first floor of the new section, was part of the development.

The architect has extended the curved form of the 1950s library into an extraordinary plan of circular shapes, which on each side are different at every level, and a complex built form which has a different appearance from every aspect. The two-storey arced wings of the library remain expressed, while the rectangular section which protrudes from the centre of the arc is incorporated in the new seven-storey building. The library's axis can be read from the Miller Street entry, but the new building sets up its own strong bipartite separation, with one half acting as a backdrop to the other. Its most strongly sculptural and dynamic side overlooks the park, with floors set back to reduce intrusion and overshadowing of the new green space, and flying buttresses to reinforce both its structure and dramatic presence. The north-facing section, also curvaceous, rises in a simple vertical plane above the recessed building entrance.

ADDRESS Miller and Ridge Streets, North Sydney
CLIENT North Sydney Council
STRUCTURAL ENGINEER Miller Milston & Ferris
SIZE 5,000 square metres
COST AUD$8.5 million including library refurbishment
ACCESS open

Northern Suburbs

Feiko Bouman Architect 1989

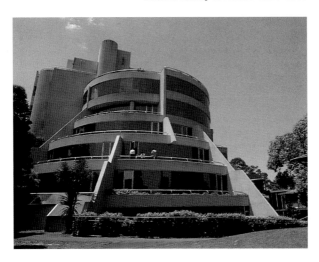

Feiko Bouman Architect 1989

SCEGGS Redlands Gymnasium

This well-known private school contains a variety of building types from various periods, including Federation cottages, converted two-storey walk-up flats and 1950s and 60s institutional classroom blocks, all laid out in an incoherent, fragmented fashion on a site of limited size. The school had no street presence or symbolic sense of place, and the architect saw the requirement for a new gymnasium as the opportunity to insert a building which would create a focus for the school and bring the other elements into a meaningful relationship with it. A tall order, but the site for the building was on the periphery of the school grounds, fronting a major road and addressing one of two entry points to the grounds.

The gymnasium was designed with an eye-catching billboard façade of deep blue (the school colour) ceramic tiles. This acts as a screen to the building's large awkward volume and also provides a contemporary signpost to the educational landmark and a unifying element behind which the various other school buildings seek common address.

The entire structure is elevated one storey off the ground to provide space for changing rooms and wet areas below. Entry to the gym is marked by a pair of formal stairs which can be seen rising from behind the screen. Inside, the gym is naturally lit through white laminated-glass strip windows, above which hovers the gracefully vaulting roof. The space is designed 'to emphasise the imagery of elegance and human movement rather than strength and force'.

ADDRESS 272 Military Road, Cremorne
CLIENT SCEGGS Redlands
STRUCTURAL ENGINEER Bond James Laron Murtagh
AREA 674 square metres COST AUD$1.1 million
ACCESS when in use

Northern Suburbs

Alex Popov Architects 1988

Northern Suburbs

Alex Popov Architects 1988

Arun Guin House

The original building, on an elevated site with views over Middle Harbour, was a single-storey, concrete-block courtyard house, built on a modular system with main façades of aluminium-framed windows interspersed with solid panels. Although modernist inspired, the house had neither spatial sophistication nor architectural merit. However, it had a well-established garden with exotic planting and tall palm trees, and a swimming pool. The client needed more space for entertaining and more bedrooms for guests. The answer to his brief is a clever conversion which, while retaining virtually all the original structure, has transformed the building from a basic, 1960s California-type bungalow to a rich, 1990s, Sydney interpretation of the Californian modernist tradition.

The architect, Ken Kennedy, set up a compositional framework for the additions in a manner reminiscent of Schindler. With the use of both horizontal and vertical cantilevered elements, and an emphasis on horizontal layering – with only the slightest suggestion of support from the various skeletal vertical members – he has created the appearance of a floating mass and articulated a sense of spatial continuity.

Expressed as pavilions, one hovering over the other, a new bedroom and studio (opening on to an expansive balcony) have been added over the living room. Downstairs, a new formal dining room has been created, and a large new living/dining area and kitchen open to a deck and the pool. The finely detailed front façade of stained cedar and glass contrasts with the play of solid mass at the entry.

ADDRESS 46A Wyong Road, Mosman
STRUCTURAL ENGINEER James Taylor & Associates
SIZE 200 square metres
ACCESS none

Northern Suburbs

Quadrant Design 1995

Done House

This house, built 'for a client who sought refuge and prospect', is primarily concerned with interior spaces and is a departure from Glenn Murcutt's more usual style of finely tuned, lyrical essays in steel and glass, in which the spatial rhythms of the landscape flow effortlessly from outside to inside. The Done House is a rectangular masonry building covering the whole site, and apart from a small, tantalising glass slot in the solid wall which runs along the public lane, its only vertical external opening is a wall of steel and glass at the northern, Chinaman's Beach end. All other communication with the external environment is from the central courtyard which, open only to the sky, is the core and essence of the house.

The plan places an accommodation unit at each end of the sloping, narrow site. These areas are linked on the eastern side by a long gallery which dominates the interior and has visual access (through a large single panel of glazing) on to a brilliant blue pool, of exactly the same length, which sits serenely in an austere courtyard. A solitary frangipani tree is its only other element. The southern unit contains the double garage, which forms the street wall and address, with a secluded sunbaking terrace above and main bedroom below, opening on to the court. The northern unit, a two-storey block, contains the main living areas (which also open on to the courtyard) and children's bedrooms below (opening on to a small verandah). The roof-top terrace has views to the beach and bay over a green planted roof above the living room. In the words of the architect, 'From even the deepest room in the house you can look through other rooms and know where you are in relation to the sea.'

Although this is not a typical Murcutt house, like all of his work it is responsive to the environment, and it is typical in its unique manipulation of light and delicacy of detailing. The butterfly-shaped, glazed roof of the

Glenn Murcutt 1992

Glenn Murcutt 1992

gallery has finely designed, electronically operated metal louvres which filter and direct light, and throughout the building beautifully detailed shutters and screens combine to give a sense of control over the volatile natural environment. Light is very important to Glenn Murcutt: 'We have to be able to make a building move, by shutters and operating elements, to reduce or increase light levels, include or exclude breeze.' In this house, the complex, visually connected arrangement of rooms focuses on the courtyard with its extraordinary light, which, reflected from the smooth white walls, gives an almost surreal stillness and calm to the space.

Originally, the exterior of the house was a splash of brilliant fauve colours – bright china-blue steelwork and sunshine yellow masonry. Recently, however, the clients decided that they preferred the architect's initial intention, and now the exterior is a purist white, interrupted only by the sleek beauty of the stainless steel downpipes.

Northern Suburbs

ADDRESS 28 Hopetoun Avenue, Chinaman's Beach, Mosman
STRUCTURAL ENGINEER James Taylor & Associates
SIZE approximately 325 square metres excluding terraces and courtyard
ACCESS none

Glenn Murcutt 1992

Glenn Murcutt 1992

Bryson House

Although Australian-born, Alex Popov's architectural training was in Denmark. His houses show the influence of his close connection with Jørn Utzon and display a relationship to the external environment which is rather different from the sense of uninterrupted spatial free-flow which is a hallmark of Australian domestic architecture. They are houses concerned with human communication rather than communication with the environment, and his interior spaces are formed to facilitate that activity. Views and the landscape are important, but they are always framed, creating for the inhabitants a visual and psychological separation between internal spaces and external vistas – a separation which reinforces the possibilities for communication within while not disallowing the potential for enjoyment and contemplation of the view.

Set on the slopes of the high land encircling an intimate bay on Sydney Harbour, this four-bedroom house is planned over three floors, with the living rooms and main bedrooms facing south. These rooms are organised around a central well of warm northern light which creates an internal balance and plays down the potential dominance of the view. The plan is essentially open, but a progression from inside to outside – through a sequence of frames, subtle changes in floor level and different characteristics of space and light – gives the interior an order and significance which are reminiscent of early Frank Lloyd Wright. Simple finishes, rust-coloured cement-rendered walls, coloured cement-rendered floors and timber joinery keep this house firmly within a contemporary idiom.

ADDRESS 7 Curlew Camp Road, Mosman
STRUCTURAL ENGINEER Bond James Norrie & Marsden
SIZE 350 square metres COST AUD$700,000
ACCESS none

Alex Popov Architects 1995

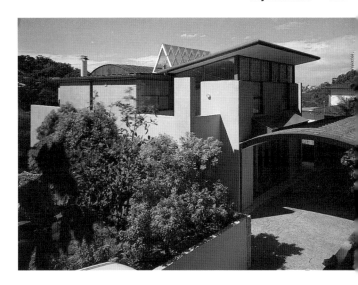

Alex Popov Architects 1995

Pair of Houses

The site for these two houses, in the heart of one of Sydney's most unadventurous, middle-class, suburban cottage belts, was steep, damp, weed-infested and south facing, with limited vehicular access. It was regarded as unsuitable for development by local government, and seemed an unlikely site for a low-cost housing project which the developer could sell from the plans and construction-manage himself. To have engaged a modern architect to design the development might seem to have compounded the gamble even further. But the success of these houses indicates that there is a market for good architecture in speculative housing development.

Each house was to have three bedrooms, two bathrooms, two car spaces and generous indoor and outdoor living areas. Statutory requirements limited the size of each house to 125 square metres, the height to two storeys, and the form to a single, attached, dual-occupancy building. The last requirement was interpreted by the architects as a complementary pair of houses sharing a common entry. The plans are inflected according to the property boundaries, the line of the cliff behind and a magnificent old angophora tree, and form a v-shaped entry court with stairs leading to the garden on top of the cliff.

In both houses lofty living rooms occupy an entire floor, located on top of bedrooms and service rooms to gain both views and sunlight. The volumes derived from the site conditions promoted two distinctive interiors. In the squarer of the two houses a uniform ceiling plane unites a regular plan, and a tiered section conceals a straight stairway which, framed by a pair of circular columns, gives entry at the middle of the room. In the longer house a stairway along the eastern wall provides a promenade around an irregular plan and a complex interlocking section. Every room in each house opens on to a balcony or terrace.

Hill Thallis Architects/Peter John Cantrill Architect 1995

Hill Thallis Architects/Peter John Cantrill Architect 1995

The structure (which limited cutting of the ground and enabled all native trees and ferns to be retained) is a bolted, steel frame of minimum weight and minimal columns braced by timber framing, cladding and flooring. Externally, the buildings are tall and thin – their height accentuated by the elevation of the front section to allow open parking below, and the addition of large, high-sided roof decks which are open only to the view and the sky.

The horizontal emphasis of balconies and windows, contrasting with the verticality of the jarrah cladding and tallow wood mullions, animates the timber and glass façades and creates a dynamic play between solid and void while blending easily into the bushy site.

ADDRESS 83 Cliff Avenue, Northbridge
CLIENT Mark Lindfield
STRUCTURAL ENGINEER Taylor Thomson Whitting
SIZE each house 200 square metres including decks
COST AUD$350,000
ACCESS none

Hill Thallis Architects/Peter John Cantrill Architect 1995

Hill Thallis Architects/Peter John Cantrill Architect 1995

Griffin House

This house is set in a suburb which Walter Burley Griffin, the American architect who won the competition to design Canberra in 1913, planned and established in the early 1920s, designing all the original houses himself. They are still there. Low-slung, flat-roofed, constructed of rough stonework, they bespeak Frank Lloyd Wright and Louis Sullivan, and now sit like precious jewels in a suburb which has been overrun by typical, dismal, suburban-Sydney housing.

The Griffin House is not one of the latter, and the architect's style and handling of space and materials are perfectly complementary, if not similar, to that of Griffin himself. On a steep south-facing site overlooking Middle Harbour, this house, constructed of deeply corbelled brickwork, consists of three pavilions (for living, dining and sleeping), connected by a columned corridor around a pool and terraces. The concept is generated by informal living, with the long corridor walk framing and capitalising on views and providing shade and a cooling breezeway. The pavilions are defined at roof level by large skylights, and at floor level a change in materials differentiates the circulation from the activity space of the rooms – marble is used for the corridor and ash parquetry for the seating and dining-table areas. All the wall cupboards – and furniture in the bedroom, kitchen and hall – are designed as part of the wallscape.

In reference to Griffin, areas of sandstone walls are included on the façade, and the external massing and colouring are purposely designed to look weathered.

ADDRESS 8 Rockley Street, Castlecrag
STRUCTURAL ENGINEER Bond James Norrie & Marsden
SIZE 450 square metres COST AUD$900,000
ACCESS none

Alex Popov Architects 1988

Alex Popov Architects 1988

Apple Computers Australian Headquarters

The building provides Apple Computers with a corporate headquarters for its Australian operations and a central distribution point for its products to the Australian market. Situated on a 2-hectare site on a high knoll, next to a main arterial road, it has distant views of Sydney's northern beaches, but is exposed to the weather, particularly from the south. Apple's brief to the architects was for an innovative, creative, accessible, egalitarian, Australian building – and this complex attempts to be all those things, with varying degrees of success.

Planned within the framework of a rectangular grid to allow for a practical arrangement of the required functions and facilitate any future change, the building houses operations on four levels, and includes a high warehouse with a southerly extension which slides under the main building, reducing its overall physical bulk. On the second level are the computer operations and repair centre; and on the third level, information technology and customer services are situated in a double-height atrium which, supported on raking, blue-painted steel trusses, features huge, vertically disposed, apple-green air-conditioning ducts and acts as a meeting place for the staff. Overlooking this space is the sales and marketing area on the fourth floor. A small training facility is placed externally at 45 degrees, next to the entry, in a free-standing ziggurat structure with a cone-shaped roof.

From the road the main building also reads as a ziggurat form. The long, low-slung, two-storey section in the foreground steps gradually up to its full four-storey height with a series of strong horizontal roof lines which are part of the system providing sunshading to the atrium. It is the sunshading and shadows which articulate the otherwise flush treatment of the whole external envelope of the building.

Allen Jack + Cottier 1987

Northern Suburbs

Allen Jack + Cottier 1987

The emphasis of structural details with bright colours is carried throughout the building, both internally and externally, and, internally, the use of curves is prevalent in the design. A blue curved wall connects the staff recreation area to the atrium, and a red curve contains an auditorium and leads the visitor towards demonstration centres behind glass-brick walls. In the cafeteria, a floor-to-ceiling glazed screen winds in and out of the structure along the southern façade. The office environment is non-hierarchical, with spaces fluid and open. A private office is provided for reasons of function only, not status.

This is an impressive building with a fundamentally modernist design which has been overlaid with an assemblage of hi-tech imagery and some post-modern elements and details. These set up contrasts and ambiguities which, although interesting and playful, tend to diminish the building's clarity and vitality.

Northern Suburbs

ADDRESS 16 Rodborough Road, Frenchs Forest
CLIENT Apple Computers Australia Corporation
STRUCTURAL ENGINEER Taylor Thomson Whitting
SIZE 10,160 square metres COST AUD$10 million
ACCESS to public areas

Allen Jack + Cottier 1987

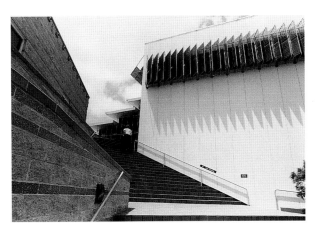

Allen Jack + Cottier 1987

Ku-ring-gai Public Library and Gordon Police Station

This development is the result of an unusual joint venture between Ku-ring-gai Council and the NSW Police Department, who were both looking for sites at the same time. The development involves the re-use of the 1876 sandstone school building to house gallery spaces, but the main functions of both library and police are contained within the new building. The scheme has been skilfully designed to allow the library to dominate, and though the police station occupies the ground floor it has a much lower profile and a separate address on a different street frontage.

The architects took advantage of the double programme and the shape of the site (which slices off at an angle along a railway cutting at the rear) to design a building which has a rigorous sense of composure externally (even if it owes a debt to some of James Stirling's work) and looks equally good on all sides. Large expanses of brickwork are broken up by the modulation of pairs of well-detailed, green-framed windows, contrasts between round, rendered columns and brick piers, and subtly projecting surfaces. With a sequence of stepped levels, the forecourt focuses attention on the entry to the library at the intersection of the old and new buildings. It is a well-handled space with a subtly designed landscape that protects it from the highway, but it is crying out for a café, or some other reason for people to use it.

ADDRESS Corner of Pacific Highway and Park Avenue, Gordon
CLIENT Ku-ring-gai Council and Gordon Police
LANDSCAPE ARCHITECT Stevens Wallman Associates
STRUCTURAL ENGINEER Flack & Kurtz Australia Pty Ltd
SIZE 4,100 square metres COST AUD$6 million

Northern Suburbs

Schwager Brooks & Partners 1994

Northern Suburbs

Schwager Brooks & Partners 1994

Pittwater

Israel House

This exquisite treehouse, the stuff of childhood dreams and the perfect answer to fantasies of a private hideaway in a natural habitat, is the house of a builder and his young son. Originally it was planned as one of three elements to be built on the site, but finally all the basic requirements of a 250-square-metre house were compressed into this one little tower. Windows became seats, floor cavities became storage bays, wall thicknesses were reduced for maximum internal space and, in the words of the architect Peter Stutchbury, 'light was forced, pushed, bled in or let in carefully to proclaim space'.

The site was a large, steeply sloping, densely vegetated block of natural bushland running down to the shores of Pittwater, and the architect's immediate response was to let the land dominate. A previous owner had cleared the area above a large rock ledge to build a house close to the road. The tower was planned to sit below this ledge, and the owner/builder had to move 30 tonnes of soil back up the slope to reclaim the site. The descent to the tower is important to the concept. It is not an easy, urban passage, but a physical, tactile experience of the natural bushland and topography.

Sitting against a backdrop of spotted gums, the tower is connected at mid-level to the edge of the rock platform by a tenuous, narrow plank bridge which, despite the incredible lightness and elegance of the structure, introduces the sense of a mini-fortress and private hideaway in the forest. From the bridge, the entry is on to a wafer-thin timber deck with no railings, which projects from the building's large northern opening and continues the fortress imagery by looking as though it could easily be snapped back into a vertical position, like a mediaeval castle gate, to prevent entry from unwelcome visitors. This is the living/dining/kitchen level, which also responds, with the design of its openings, to the expanse

Stutchbury and Pape 1993

Stutchbury and Pape 1993

of Pittwater revealed through the trees, and to the sight and sounds of an on-site waterfall.

The lower level of the tower is on the rock ledge. Built of concrete blockwork and containing the laundry/bathroom, it is meant to feel 'wet and dark'. The upper, bedroom level looks through tree tops to the horizon, and the roof, also an unbelievably thin slither, hovers way above window-sill level (the last area of solid wall), following the slope of the land and the path of the winter sun. All three levels were designed to be specific in their function and to optimise and create associations and relationships with aspects of the site.

The lower-level blockwork core was built on to the ground on two sides, and the stud wall system of the lightweight, exposed post-and-beam tower structure is clad with a skin made up of 12-millimetre plantation board, building paper and fibre cement, all within the tolerance of the dimensions of the posts. A single skin, two-and-a-half-storey service core of plywood vertical boards acts as the structure for the southern wall.

This seemingly simple house, with every detail carefully considered and designed by the architect, reflects not only the life of the client, but also the successful collaboration of client and architect in both the design and construction processes.

ADDRESS Avalon
STRUCTURAL ENGINEER Eva Tihanyi
SIZE 65.3 square metres
COST AUD$87,000
ACCESS telephone architect for appointment to view: (02) 9979 5030

Stutchbury and Pape 1993

Stutchbury and Pape 1993

Aubort House

Covered with spotted gums and casuarinas, the site of the Aubort House slopes dramatically at an angle of 34 degrees, from a large outcrop of boulders on the ridge-line boundary above Clareville Beach to a shorter boundary on the street. The building is located towards the centre of the site where grey concrete blockwork, a material which the architect uses for its sympathetic blending with the bush and rocks, creates a square two-storey core with 6-metre sides. Containing guest room and laundry at ground level and main bedroom above, the core serves as bracing for the rest of the building – a timber and glass platform perched on top and overhanging 3 metres beyond the base all the way round.

The living area is placed over the core with a blockwork hearth emerging from the mass below. The kitchen and family room are to the north, the dining room to the south and, to the west, the projecting area becomes a large, shaded verandah which shields the living space from the summer sun and accommodates a constant flow of activities, expanding the opportunities for adaptive living to an optimum. The architect likens this arrangement to a bush camp with its central fire creating the space for activities to occur around it. A full-width timber bridge projects from the eastern side forming a large outdoor deck, which bedrooms and bathroom open on to, in an arm extending from the dining room.

This is an evocative interpretation of the traditional verandah house, commonly built in the area before the 1950s, boldly elevated into the bush landscape.

ADDRESS 33 Hilltop Road, Clareville
STRUCTURAL ENGINEER Eva Tihanyi
SIZE 260 square metres COST AUD$280,000
ACCESS none

Pittwater

Stutchbury and Pape 1995

Stutchbury and Pape 1995

Ambler McCawley House

This complete refurbishment has turned a small two-storey timber cottage into a contemporary house with a steel structure. With a site rising steeply to the north, the original house took advantage of ocean views to the south but had no northern sun penetration. The new plan focused on getting light and winter sun into the interior while maintaining the spectacular views.

A 2-metre-wide, glass-roofed stair was added to the back of the existing house, changing the spatial focus of the plan and becoming an important light source for the existing, middle-level living area. The main roof, a large skillion with a 3-metre overhang running virtually parallel to the slope of the land, also lets northern light and sun into the new upper level with high clerestory glazing. The overhang protects the glazed roof of the stair from the hot summer sun. The white metal louvre walls of the stair are opened in summer, allowing cross ventilation to the upper floor which, extending beyond the stair with a smaller, lower skillion roof, contains bedrooms, a large sitting room and a deck.

The form of the building, although deliberately manipulated to follow the topography, has its own dynamism and reads as a series of flying roofs, giving one the expectation that they may become airborne at any moment, in the manner of the many hangliders which are often seen in the area against a backdrop of sky, sea and cliffs. Corrugated-metal cladding was chosen for its zero maintenance and its ability to give a homogeneous form. Handrails, gutters and downpipes are of stainless steel.

ADDRESS 5 Bungen Head Road, Newport
STRUCTURAL ENGINEER Taylor Thomson Whitting
SIZE 360 square metres
ACCESS none

Pittwater

Grose Bradley 1995

Grose Bradley 1995

Friend House

The precipitous site for this holiday house has incredible views to the east over the ocean and straight up the thin spit of land which culminates in the Barrenjoey headland and lighthouse and separates Pittwater from the Pacific Ocean. The architects sought to take maximum advantage of the spectacular but difficult site, while practising restraint in the use of colour and materials so as to minimise impact on the hillside.

Set entirely below the road to comply with height regulations, the timber-clad house has roof-top car parking with million-dollar views. It comprises two pavilions, of two and three storeys, suspended on a light, steel structure which rises from various levels of the site. The pavilions are set askew, with a central staircase connecting all floors; this generates an extraordinary sequence of visual sensations, and an orchestrated variety of outlooks to both within and beyond the internal spaces. The larger northern pavilion is rectangular and contains a small study and vast roof-top deck on one level. The living room and kitchen below open on to another spacious timber deck on the northern and eastern sides, and there is a paved outdoor/indoor space on the natural ground level below. The smaller, square pavilion contains bedrooms, all with large projecting balconies, and bathrooms. Despite the topography, living spaces easily integrate with small outdoor garden spaces and paths down to the beach.

Careful consideration has been given to sun protection and the tempering of daylight with operable vertical and horizontal screens. The external walls are grey-stained timber boarding.

ADDRESS 7 Northview Road, Palm Beach
STRUCTURAL ENGINEER Demlakian Consulting Engineers
SIZE 300 square metres
ACCESS none

Pittwater

Gordon & Vallich Architects 1994

Pittwater

Gordon & Vallich Architects 1994

Roberts House

This three-storey addition, large enough to be a house in its own right, was built entirely underneath an existing building on a steeply sloping site overlooking the ocean at Palm Beach. The original 1960s flat-roofed, one-storey house extended out uncompromisingly from the flat land at street level, supported on four large, brick cross-columns, 12–15 metres high. At the front, on the northern elevation, the addition fills up the space between these columns, and at the sides it slides out beyond them under the horizontal slab form of the earlier structure. The result is an extremely unusual visual arrangement and reads as two quite different buildings – one contained in the underbelly of the other.

Though carefully considered and finely designed, the new building, with its roof 2.5 metres below the floor of the original, appears compressed and constrained by the dominating, unflinching certainties of the older one above. But internally the addition has a life of its own. Its roof forms an observation deck, with a large, glass, central pyramid giving light and height to the floors below. On the first floor, bedrooms with private balconies are oriented around a wide gallery which surrounds the large, square central void. The informal living area on the ground floor is a dynamic space with an internal focus created by the volume and light of the central void. That focus is challenged only by the view of Palm Beach, dramatically framed by the steel portal that supports the roof and contributes to the complex articulation of the front façade.

ADDRESS 16 Florida Road, Palm Beach
SIZE 250 square metres COST AUD$400,000
ACCESS none – best viewed from the southern end of the cul-de-sac road at Palm Beach

Pittwater

Alex Popov Architects 1995

Pittwater

Alex Popov Architects 1995

Pittwater House

This single-level holiday house stands on a sloping bushland site with views through tall eucalyptus trees to the Pacific Ocean and Pittwater. Over a simple rectangular building form its spectacular roof rises from the solid, street-facing wall in a long, undulating wave which, from its highest point, curls down over the side of the house and forms weather-protection for the continuous glass walls and main terrace. A reverse wave sweeps up over the carport, giving the house a memorable street presence and making progression to the glazed entry doors a dramatic experience.

An almost Miesian plan divides day and night uses by an opening in the roof, opposite the central entry and above a floor-to-ceiling glazed wall. The well floods the space with light and the window captures the first views. Spaces are formed between opposing blade walls, which extend through walls of continuous, frameless glass, obliterating corners and blurring the boundary between interior and exterior. The open living room and kitchen are to the left of the entry, and three bedrooms, a study and bathrooms are to the right. Three outdoor areas further expand the interior, creating extended visual boundaries which, with curved walls, transform the rectilinear sense of the plan.

The steel structure has a grid of columns supporting the curved roof beams, steel purlins and corrugated-metal sheeting. The walls are split concrete blocks and white masonry, and the polished-concrete flooring on an insulated concrete slab creates an effective thermal bank. Large opening glass panels in the bedrooms allow the illusion of sleeping out.

ADDRESS 21 Cynthia Road, Palm Beach
STRUCTURAL ENGINEER Birzulis Associates
SIZE 240 square metres
ACCESS none

Harry Seidler & Associates 1994

Harry Seidler & Associates 1994

Cottage Point House

Bruce Rickard was a prominent member of the Sydney School, the group of young architects who in the 1960s practised an organic architecture inspired by the work of Frank Lloyd Wright. With a palette of timber, brick and stone they designed houses which seemed to grow out of the landscape – and often let it in. Flat roofs, wide eaves, earthy open-plan interiors with clerestory windows, exposed beams and big stone fireplaces were the hallmarks of the school and Bruce Rickard created some of its best work. Thirty years on he continues to design buildings which relate intimately to their natural surroundings.

This house, on a steep site covered with tall, slim, lemon-scented gums, has fine views over the Hawkesbury River. It was built progressively from 1985, originally for the architect himself, as a substantial alteration to a modest fibro holiday cottage. Although it is in the manner of his early work, this house is lighter and even more elegant, with two timber decks elevated above the ground on timber posts, projecting in two arms to a grove of trees. The house is tied back into the ground by bedrooms and bathrooms which form the base of a U-shaped plan. One of the decks is entirely open – an outdoor living platform; the other (containing living and dining spaces and kitchen) has walls which can be opened up on the north-east and north-west sides to accentuate the experience of living in the landscape.

Unusually for this architect, the house has a pitched roof, which is used to create the spatial quality of sloping, cathedral ceilings.

ADDRESS 2 Cottage Point Road, Cottage Point
STRUCTURAL ENGINEER Taylor Lauder Consultants
SIZE 222 square metres COST AUD$195,000
ACCESS none

Pittwater

Bruce Rickard and Associates 1985–1992

Bruce Rickard and Associates 1985–1992

Index

Sydney: a guide to recent architecture

Sydney: a guide to recent architecture

Sydney: a guide to recent architecture

Sydney: a guide to recent architecture

Sydney: a guide to recent architecture

Photographs are by Stephen Dupont, except:

pages 23, 203: Farhid Assassi
pages 213, 215: Tom Balfour of Max Dupain & Associates
pages 93, 113, 121, 219: Patrick Bingham-Hall
page 153: Brett Boardman
pages 265, 273: Craig Carlstrom
page 249: Conybeare Morrison
page 61: Scott Frances
page 193: Hansen Gales
page 125: Walter Glover
pages 33, 53, 71, 73, 75, 155, 167, 201, 243, 245, 249, 253, 255: John Gollings
page 115: Margaret Krempff
page 39: Peddle Thorp Architects
1page 185: Powerhouse Museum Photography Department
page 303: Bruce Rickard
pages 49, 87, 98, 135, 259, 261: Eric Sierens of Max Dupain & Associates